IN RAJASTHAN

Royina Grewal

LONELY PLANET PUBLICATIONS
Melbourne • Oakland • London • Paris

In Rajasthan

Published by Lonely Planet Publications

Head Office: PO Box 617, Hawthorn, Vic 3122, Australia
Branches: 155 Filbert St, Suite 251, Oakland, CA 94607, USA
              10 Barley Mow Passage, Chiswick, London W4 4PH, UK
              71 bis rue du Cardinal Lemoine, 75005 Paris, France

Published 1997

Printed by SNP Printing Pte Ltd, Singapore

Author photograph by Ashok Dilwali, Kinsey Bros
Map by Adam McCrow

National Library of Australia Cataloguing in Publication Data

Grewal, Royina
In Rajasthan

ISBN 0 86442 457 4.

1. Grewal, Royina – Journeys – Rajasthan (India).
2. Rajasthan (India) – Description and travel.
3. Rajasthan (India) – Social life and customs. I. Title.
(Series: Lonely Planet Journeys.)

915.4404052

Text © Royina Grewal 1997
Map © Lonely Planet 1997

For our three children

ACKNOWLEDGMENTS

This book is the product of the time and words shared so generously with me by the hundreds of people I met all over Rajasthan. To my enormous regret I have been able to include only a tiny fraction of these encounters; the contribution made by each, however, remains present in many nuances throughout the book.

My special thanks to Lalit Shah, who presided over the book's beginnings with a gift of Todd's *Annals and Antiquities of Rajasthan*, and to Aman Nath, who allowed me access to his remarkable books on Rajasthan. Fauzia and Durru Loharu gave me a home at Jaipur and much inspiration. Yaduvendra Sahai of Jaipur's City Palace Museum provided reams of information that enlarged my understanding of Rajasthan. Kesri Singh and Arvind Sharma at Mandava were generous with their time and hospitality. Mahendra Singh (Monty) at Jodhpur allowed me insights into his remarkable mind and put to rest many misconceptions about Rajputs. Narendra Singh Bhati, also at Jodhpur, is another old friend who came to my rescue in many different ways. Rajendra Singh of Rajasthan Tourism at Bikaner, and so many other tourism officers, taught me to see and not to judge. Sanjit and Navneet Ohri of Continental Computers, Delhi, kept my temperamental machine going, and Ashish Gulhati introduced me to the marvels of cyber space. I thank them all. I am also indebted to Rajasthan Tourism, the Rajasthan Tourism Development Corporation and Welcome Group Hotels for the support and assistance I received.

I had planned this journey through Rajasthan for years, but it was Michelle de Kretser, publisher of Lonely Planet's Journeys series, who finally urged me to take it. Her unflagging enthusiasm helped sustain my own, and her encouragement and friendship kept me going through the lonely and often frustrating process of writing. I have also been particularly fortunate with my editor, Janet Austin, who ploughed through various versions of the manuscript with cheerful fortitude, bringing skill, sympathy and sensitivity to her often difficult task. Through Michelle, Janet and Ravi Singh in Delhi, who edited my previous book, I now understand that writers produce manuscripts – editors convert them into books. Bless them all.

And finally there is my long-suffering family, who put up with my absences, both physical and mental. Writers less fortunate would have had to stay responsibly at home.

CONTENTS

PREFACE

THREE YEARS ago my husband, Ajit, decided to opt out of the corporate world to work in agricultural and rural development. Much to my delight, we moved from Bombay to a small farm (without running water or reliable electricity supply) in the village of Patan, in the Alwar district of north-eastern Rajasthan. Ajit now works with marginal farmers, teaching them agricultural and horticultural techniques to optimise their earnings. Since I have only to look at a plant for it to die, I restrict myself to the social aspects of rural development and continue to write.

Although the move to Patan was a huge jump from one civilisation to another, and it took us a while to settle into our new world, tuning in to rural rhythms was easy. Since it's impossible to accelerate the growth of plants, we have learnt to slow down. Our frenetic city edge has gradually worn off, and our thought processes have become sharper and clearer.

Our living conditions too are, well, different. We live in a two-room shack of stone and lime mortar that the ladies from the village have unanimously proclaimed far inferior to their homes. But we do have a pool, a nice large one which started out as a water storage tank for Ajit's irrigation system. We are slowly building a rather unconventional house – a sequence of domes, well suited to our climate – which is being constructed in the old way, without steel or cement.

We chose to live in Rajasthan because Ajit wanted to launch his agricultural experiment on the most unproductive land he could find. When we bought the land at Patan it was typical Rajasthani wasteland: undulating sandy dunes littered with a few patches of tall *sarkanda* grass, a drab palette of beiges and browns that sucked water greedily. The entire forty acres had only a single tree; today there are around sixty-five thousand.

To demonstrate the optimal use of land, Ajit planted fruit trees and grew traditional crops between them. The land slowly revived. The birds came back: partridge, quail and especially peacock, exotic symbols of Rajasthan. Jackals returned too, attracted by the peacocks as well as by our watermelons, to which they are apparently passionately addicted.

Our interaction with the local people increased and gradually the caste composition of the village became clear. It is a hierarchy in which each person has a defined place and a specific duty to the community. We began to appreciate how the much-reviled caste system honed traditional skills, from generation to generation; however, we also empathised with those who wished to exchange the hereditary occupations of the past for a future where anything is possible.

And things were beginning to change, even in our remote

village. Shortly after our move to Patan, local elections were announced for the positions of *sarpanch*, the heads of the administrative bodies governing small groups of villages in the region. Patan was reserved for women candidates only – a small revolution, especially in rural Rajasthan, where education is meagre and a woman's position in society is determined by that of her husband. Shakuntala, the wife of the village money-lender, decided to stand as a candidate. Overnight she was transformed from a veiled, subservient woman to an individual in her own right, with a possible political future. The transformation extended also to her band of women supporters.

The group travelled through the region, perched on a tractor, shouting slogans through megaphones and generally having the time of their lives. But Shakuntala lost the election. I went to commiserate and found the women in attitudes of despair. During our conversation an idea germinated. Why waste the energy and enthusiasm generated during the elections? Why not channel it to form a women's organisation that would work towards making Patan a model village, the envy of the district? A women's group was duly formed. Its various schemes include family planning, tree planting and the opening of a crèche, all operating by self-sustaining means, depending as little as possible on outside finance.

Despite the activities of our women's group, I was at a bit of a loose end in Patan. I had just finished a book on the Narmada, a

13

lissom river that I had followed through central India, and was tossing around ideas for a new book, but somehow none of the subjects or destinations I considered inspired me. And then it struck me: here I was, living on the fringe of India's most exotic state, and yet my experience of it was terribly limited. My trips over the years had taken me to various parts of Rajasthan, but only very superficially. I had met a vast range of people – Maharajas, game wardens, folk musicians, social workers, artists, historians – but I had never had sufficient time to follow the leads they provided, to draw out their individual stories.

I began to read everything I could find on Rajasthan's history and distinctive geology. The land had only relatively recently become desert, and had nurtured sophisticated civilisations over two thousand years before Christ. I read of the original inhabitants, the Mina and Bhil tribes, who were pushed into the Aravalli hills and marginalised by successive waves of settlers who established small kingdoms and came to call themselves Rajputs (from *rajputras*, or sons of kings). The settlers created elaborate genealogies to endorse their power and prestige, some tracing their ancestry to deities or hero kings of sacred literature, to the sun, the moon or the sacred fire.

The fierce Rajputs fought endlessly amongst themselves for control of this strategically positioned arid land, which lay astride vital trade and military routes. Armies marched across the desert, and battles were fought over handfuls of dust. Caravans laden with riches also crossed the barren wastes and paused to rest and trade at the great markets that grew up along the route. I traced their passage across the map with longing.

Inevitably, I encountered Captain James Todd, who documented the land and its people in the three exhaustive volumes of his *Annals and Antiquities of Rajasthan*, published in 1829. This paean to Rajput heroism has dominated subsequent opinions and attitudes, perhaps even those of the Rajputs themselves.

Todd came to India in 1778 as a sixteen-year-old cadet in the employ of the British East India Company. In 1818 he was appointed political agent of western Rajasthan, charged with the task of persuading the Rajput kingdoms to enter into treaties with the Company. He came to admire the Rajputs' loyalty and gallantry, qualities which were sustained by the glorious martial traditions of their past. Todd's passionate belief in their potential as loyal allies to British interests in India attracted criticisms of partiality and eventually hastened his return to England.

I had always been interested in the Rajput psyche, but was ambivalent about the myth of chivalry and honour that lay at the root of Todd's romantic interpretation. When Todd observed the Rajputs they had already compromised their much-vaunted honour through more than two hundred years of indulgent vassalage to the Moghuls. And later, when Maratha warriors from the west coast began to raid their territories and extort enormous taxes, the Rajputs accepted a closer union with the British, surrendering all but the vestiges of sovereignty. They were left with only the trappings of power: their courts, their titles and a preoccupation with honour which hid an essential emptiness.

Despite their increasing exposure to the West, thanks to education at Eton and Harrow, Oxford and Cambridge, the princes – the title to which the Rajputs had been reduced –

remained suspended between past and present. Their magnificent palaces, stables of cars and extravagant lifestyles were hollow attempts to escape reality. Indian Independence further undermined what was left of their stature when the states were merged with the Indian Union, and the final blow came in 1971 with the withdrawal of privy purse stipends.

The abolition of the privy purse occurred when, to my way of thinking, I was an intelligent adult. I welcomed the ending of this anachronism, of the waste of taxing our hard-earned money to support lifestyles which were completely out of step with India's socialist structure. In my post-college, left-wing idealism, I ignored the fact that when the princely states merged with the Indian Union, many contributed their entire exchequer to the new nation. Moreover, the privy purse did not only sustain the Maharajas' lavish lifestyles, but also supported the scores of people who had been dependent on them and their families for generations: the craftsmen, the entertainers, the armies of personal retainers and the children of multiple wives.

My feelings of ambivalence deepened, however, when I considered Rajput machismo and the subjugation of women by such offensive traditions as *purdah*, the veiling and seclusion of women; *jauhar*, the mass suicide by immolation committed by women when defeat was imminent; and, worst of all, *sati*, whereby women were immolated on the funeral pyres of their husbands. These customs were perpetuated for reasons of honour, but they also served well to keep women in their place.

Since more than half of Rajasthan is made up of arid wasteland which cannot sustain settled populations, nomadism continues to be a way of life for many thousands of people. Whenever I have met any of these people, I have been drawn to them, but I was particularly inspired by the nomadic Rabari herdsman who arrived in Patan one day to deliver my surprise birthday present: two camels!

The herdsman had been on the road for months, and his quest for fodder would keep him on the move for several more. Constantly faced with the reality of drought, he had no option but to wander. He spoke longingly of his desert homeland: the vast expanses, the silences and the muted beiges and browns that are so soothing to the eye, unlike the strident greens of other places.

'The desert is like a beautiful woman,' he said dreamily, 'whose beauty and purity shines through. She does not need ornaments of greenery.'

The Rabari's reminiscences triggered off a flood of memories, for as a child I'd had an almost obsessive fascination with the desert. I had eagerly listened to adult conversations about the desert encroaching on Delhi, when trees had been planted feverishly and green belts established to arrest its progress. The shifting desert became for me a real, living entity, a menacing creature that men sought to entrap in greenery. My obsession had persisted even after my marriage. I was entranced by Ajit's description of a trip he had once made to Jaisalmer, when the road he had taken had been obliterated by the desert: dunes on the left of the road in the morning had shifted to the right by evening.

My imagination was stirred further when a group of Gaduliya Lohars came into our region. These nomadic blacksmiths travel through Rajasthan in beautifully worked metal carts, stopping off to tend to the needs of the villages they pass. To me they symbolise the quixotism of the Rajputs. Originally the armourers of Chittor, famed for the strong, sharp blades they forged, they abandoned the legendary citadel after it was conquered by the Moghuls, swearing never to return until it was recaptured. At Independence, the Gaduliya Lohars were offered land and the opportunity to settle, but most preferred their wandering life. Now, almost fifty years later, they regret their decision. If they were settled their children could go to school, but their numbers have multiplied and it is too late to make good the promised land allotments.

The Gaduliya Lohars' camp site, squeezed into a vacant piece of land between the road and our village, was crowded with their distinctive carts, every surface covered in handworked brass. The carts were home to nearly thirty families, and had been used to travel around the country for generations. There were string beds in many of them, and they were surrounded by goats, dogs and bright-eyed children.

Guler Singh was working the bellows beside the cart closest to the road, his seamed face shaded by an intricately coiled red turban. He wore an old plaid shirt, a fluid *dhoti* and lots of jewellery: brass earrings, necklaces of shining glass beads and a large beaten-brass bangle. He barely looked up at me as he worked on the griddle he was making over glowing coals. From time to time he puffed energetically at his bellows, studying the flame and the colour of the iron, and when both were perfect he signalled to his very pregnant wife to pound the iron with a huge mallet. Iron rang on iron, until he stopped her with a sign and heated the griddle some more. She pounded again, and the process continued until both were satisfied. Only then did Guler Singh acknowledge my presence.

'It was a crucial stage,' he apologised, straightening up painfully. 'The heating must be just right, and so it was vital that I concentrate on the exact colour of the coals to gauge the temperature. I have to be confident that what I produce is of fine quality. We still pride ourselves on excellence, even if we no longer make swords and spears and shields and arrow shafts.'

He paused, squinting at a match as he lit a *bidi*. 'Now we make axes and ploughshares, agricultural implements and household utensils,' he said wryly. 'It's a far cry from our days of glory but at least we survive.'

But I knew that the living they made was far from adequate. With the increasing use of mass-produced, factory-made implements and utensils, few people now bought their wares.

'Is it not time to return to Chittor?' I asked. 'Your ancestors' vow is history. Can't it be set aside?'

Guler Singh drew himself erect. 'The word of a Rajput is a pledge for all eternity,' he declared fiercely.

Time was money and food for the family, I realised, and so I reluctantly made my farewells.

'Why don't you come back and visit us later?' Guler Singh suggested. 'Nights are best, because we are free from work.'

'But come within the next couple of days,' his wife warned

me, 'because then we leave for Tijara.'

An idea began to form in my mind, and I asked if I could travel at least part of the way with them. 'In our carts!' they laughed incredulously. I persisted and they finally agreed.

I arrived on the designated day to find their carts being loaded into small trucks. 'What on earth is going on?' I asked Guler Singh's wife.

'We're moving,' she said, 'as we discussed. Now, which truck are you going to take?'

I spluttered with confusion. 'But where are the bullocks . . . the bullocks to pull the carts?'

'What bullocks? They're far too expensive for the likes of us. And they've got to be fed, you know, and that too costs money. That's why we have the trucks. Now, choose which one you'd like.'

I stood by, stupefied. This wasn't the journey I had wanted to make. Bullock carts in trucks! An entire way of life was passing and we didn't even know it.

The encounter with the Gaduliya Lohars had taught me a significant lesson about the danger of nurturing stereotyped images of Rajasthan and its people. The time had come for me to discover what lay behind the exotic façades and experience the larger reality of what was now my home state.

I started to make serious travel plans. Everyone was an expert on Rajasthan; friends bombarded me with advice, places I simply must see and people whom it was essential to meet. My lists expanded every day, until I tore them all up and started afresh. The six weeks that I had mentally set aside for the journey expanded to eight. It was impossible to arrive at a comprehensive itinerary, and it would take a lifetime to experience all of Rajasthan. I began to envisage a more subjective, personal journey.

I decided to head in the general direction of the desert and take in as many places as possible on the way. I longed to experience the desert for myself, to see the great Thar with its golden sand and windswept dunes. Our little patch of desert in Patan, now greened beyond recognition, was certainly sandy but it was far from being the desert of my imaginings. My desert was a vast, empty expanse of sand, where howling winds sculpted enormous dunes; it stood for the sheer personal indulgence of wandering, of irresponsibility and non-accountability. It stood for the nomadic life that I craved.

CHAPTER 1
ALWAR

I LEAVE PATAN and Ajit with some regret, but there is also that wonderful bright-eyed and bushy-tailed feeling that accompanies the beginning of a journey. It seems as though the world has been created anew, and I see with great clarity and precision.

A fine drizzle lifts my spirits further and follows me from Patan to the Delhi–Jaipur road, and all the way to Neemrana. I have decided to stop at the Neemrana Fort Palace, the most ancient heritage hotel in the country. It opened in 1986 to rave reviews of its sensitive restoration, and since the transition from palace to heritage hotel marks an important phase in the life of present-day Rajasthan, it seems appropriate to start off my travels in this way.

The rain has washed the dust from the trees, which are now a shining green, and the earth is refreshed. Some boys are playing in a puddle beside the road – shining, brown bodies and bright, happy eyes. The cattle they are tending are soaking wet but grazing with contentment. My heart soars.

Perhaps you have to live in India to respond to the rain as we do. It is a deep gut response, as much in relief from the heat as in recognition of the life-giving properties of water. Rain means crops, which mean life. But I also think it has something to do with a softening of the light; we have so much sun, blue sky and blinding glare. An entire aesthetic evolved around rain in Rajasthani art and literature; in music there are *ragas* to induce rain, and poetry describes rainy days as being conducive to erotic longings.

December is a perfect time of the year to be travelling. The mustard, a relatively new crop to Rajasthan, is just beginning to flower, and we drive past enveloped in its delicate fragrance. Wisps of cloud drift low across the stunted outcrops of the Aravalli hills. I am reminded of one of Ajit's farmers who once told me that the clouds come down at night to 'drink' water, and as a result often become heavy-bellied and slow to rise. A shaft of sunlight struggles through the clouds to spotlight a field of tender new wheat. Mahavir, my driver, sums it up: 'The earth has put on all her ornaments.'

As we pass roadside villages, I notice that many women's faces are heavily veiled by their long and wide *odhnis*, the ends of which are tossed over their shoulders without even a perfunctory attempt being made to cover their breasts with folds of the fabric. I recall my friend Shakuntala from Patan chuckling wickedly about these women. 'You never see their faces,' she had said. 'The only way to recognise them is by the shape of their breasts.' We had spoken about the issue of veiling, and had come to the conclusion that the richer the family and the higher the caste, the greater the seclusion of women.

The Delhi–Jaipur road is an arterial highway which bristles with commerce, and we are following a stream of trucks loaded with everything from tiers of spanking-new cars to cartons of detergent. I have always been fascinated by the attention truck drivers pay to the decoration of their vehicles: paintings of auspicious motifs such as lotuses, birds and cows cover the bodywork; glittering decorations dangle from the front and rear bumpers; and in the driver's cabin there are icons of the gods and pin-ups of scantily clad women. Best of all are the little homilies painted on the back of the trucks. The lettering on one loaded with bananas reads: 'Oh you of the evil eye, may your face be blackened'. Just a little further on there is a happier variation: 'Even you of the evil eye, may God bless you'. A third advises: 'Regard the world with love, remember you take nothing with you when you die'. Death indeed rides with the truckies, whose vehicles are often dangerously overloaded. The edge of the road is littered with battered wrecks, memorials to drivers who drove too far, for too long. But most truck drivers drive slowly and well: their lives depend on it.

Neemrana's fort is concealed in a horseshoe-shaped formation of the Aravalli hills. It was constructed in 1494 and named for Nimole Meo, a brave chieftain defeated by the Chauhan Rajputs, who respected his plea that his name remain associated with his lost kingdom. Signs direct us off the main road and onto a narrow track that is in the process of completing its transition to a road. Finally, around a bend, the fort soars above us – a cliff of dun-coloured masonry with crenellated bastions, and rising above it, the many-tiered palace, punctuated with pillared balconies and fretted stone lattices. Impressive, formidable and also faintly mysterious.

Since it is still the off season, the hotel is not fully occupied and I wander through a series of rooms, each restored with simplicity and restraint. I finally decide to take Badal Mahal, palace of the clouds, appropriate for this rainy day. It is high up on the eighth floor, overlooking forested hillsides. Low clouds drift past the windows and in the distance more rain approaches.

Later in the afternoon I wander through the palace exploring its many terraces. A sudden downpour, and I seek shelter in a large pillared room where a tailor is bent over his machine. He is a wizened old man, peering through thick glasses at his work: uniforms of maroon *kurtas* and *pyjama* for Neemrana's staff. He is happy to have a visitor and chats animatedly about the old days when the Raja lived at Neemrana.

'I don't remember too much,' he says. 'The Raja moved into the village when I was still a child. What I do remember are the trees of glass that used to decorate all the rooms.'

I don't understand what he means.

'You know, the kind that grow from the ceiling,' he says, and I realise that he is referring to chandeliers.

We talk about the differences between life under the Maharajas and life today. 'Well, it's true no-one dies of hunger any more,' he says thoughtfully. 'The new hybrid seeds and the availability of water give us better crops than ever before. And those that are employed earn huge salaries. So everyone has enough.' He looks into the distance with rheumy eyes.

'But . . .' I prompt.

'But no-one listens to your problems any more. In the days of the Maharaja you could go to the ruler and tell him your difficulty, and if it was genuine he would do everything he could to help you. Today, for every little thing you have to meet with some clerk in a government office.'

It used to be like the relationship of a father and a son: there was a closeness. He was their Raja and they his children. They may not have liked each other very much but they felt responsible for each other. It never ceases to amaze me how the ordinary people, whose taxes partly supported the extravagant lifestyles of the rulers, who in turn had more in common with life on the Riviera than with their subjects, were still bound by reciprocal bonds. When there was a marriage in the village, the Raja would send gifts of money; when there was a death, the wood for the funeral pyre would be provided by the palace. Government was embodied in a single person whose actions conformed with tradition and were on a human scale. This was possible because of the much smaller size of their kingdoms. Size is one of modern India's chief problems: it brings distance and impersonality.

Aman Nath, one of the owners of Neemrana, joins me for tea. He is a slight man, with a burning intensity and an elegant manner. When he and his partners took over the palace it was in ruins, inhabited by bats and mice. It took five years of hard work and round-the-clock attention before a few rooms were ready to be opened to the public.

'We worked particularly hard on the bathrooms,' Aman says,

'and tried to give each a view, sometimes multiple views, so that when you are bathing you can look out. It's something we considered most important.'

Aman shows me an article he has written on Neemrana, titled 'Loos with Views'. 'Most hotels,' he points out, 'depend on linear access through corridors so the bedroom naturally monopolises the view, and the bathroom, neatly functional, is tucked into a convenient, but often dark, corner.'

The *pièce de résistance* is the bathroom of the Shringar Mahal, where the Maharanis adorned themselves. Guests often discover its open-air bathroom with a mixture of shocked delight and coyness: a louvred grill provides a view of the village from the toilet, while the shower stands among green shrubs and trees, with the ever-changing Rajasthani sky above.

We speak with regret about the rapidly disappearing magic of the toilette. 'The shower and the pace of life have changed everything,' Aman says sadly. 'Bathrooms have become antiseptic and functional. They even look alike in most hotels.'

I ask Aman what attracted him to Rajasthan. 'It is like an opera or film set,' he replies. 'All the actors have left the stage, and the set is partly dismantled.'

'And the Rajputs?' I prompt.

'They are like the extras.'

In the evening, Aman and I take our drinks on a terrace enclosed by spires and domes etched against clouds radiant with the golden colours of the setting sun. He shares the experience of his early attempts at social work in the Neemrana village.

'One of the things we discovered, to our city-bred horror, was that no house in the village had piped water. The women all had to walk to the well twice a day. So we decided to give the village a piped water system. We were spending so much on the renovations, a little more wouldn't make too much difference, and anyway, we felt we wanted to do something for the village.'

Surveys were made of water needs, pipe lengths and so on. Then early one morning while Aman was lingering over his breakfast in the sun, a group of women from the village came to see him. They were evidently deeply distressed, so Aman sat them down and asked what was the matter.

'The piped water,' one had said. 'You are destroying our lives,' another had added. Aman laughs at the memory of his complete mystification. Slowly, the difficulty had been explained.

'You see,' the most articulate of the group had said, 'collecting water from the well twice a day is not a chore for us. In fact it is a welcome outing when all of us can gather together and chat. It gets us out of the house and gives us a break from routine. We gossip, we laugh, we have fun. And now you want to take this all away from us with your stupid schemes of piped water. What are you trying to do, make us prisoners in our homes?'

I am reminded of our own efforts at Patan. We too made similar mistakes, all with the very best of intentions, but according to our own concepts of social responsibility. The mistake we all made was to allow our own set of values to influence our perception of the needs of the people. We should have asked *them* what their needs were. Development agencies all over India are making the same mistake and wasting huge amounts of time and money on projects people do not need or want. Aman and his associates eventually drilled another well for the village, a sweet water well to supplement the brackish water in the existing one, but in consultation with the people.

A detour off the Jaipur highway takes us to Alwar, in modern times an important satellite town to Delhi, and historically the gateway to Rajasthan. The car labours up and down the shoulders of ancient hills, hidden among which, craggy and splintered, sit innumerable little forts on impossibly inaccessible peaks. These forts were all once controlled by the Meo tribes, whose dominions stretched from the area around Patan, beyond Alwar and all the way to Ajmer.

My attention is focused upwards, and as Alwar approaches I see its battlements contoured along the highest points of the undulating hills. They look like the spine of some long-decayed monster. We pass watchtowers at frequent intervals, stern sentinels guarding the approach to the city. I respond strongly to monuments but I'm basically a fort person, and Alwar's, Bala Quila, is a gem. We go straight up.

Forts, to me, are statements of defence and defiance, but also of prosperity – of rich lands protected from intruders. They conjure up the pageantry of medieval kingship, the movement of armies, the shrill of trumpets and the tread of soldiers. I tend to forget that greed often supported these lifestyles, and that

29

blood, pain and grief were the backdrop.

There is hectic activity at Bala Quila as scores of citizens, including hordes of school children, remove rubble and undergrowth from the forecourt. The Collector of Alwar, Manohar Kant Sharma, and his wife, Sarita, are among them. The Collector, who is also the administrative head of the district, is a small, dapper man, with a brisk, no-nonsense air. The restoration he has instigated is the most effective conservation project I have ever seen. The involvement and commitment of the people to their own heritage moves me greatly. Purists would probably be horrified by the amateurishness of the undertaking, and some mistakes will inevitably occur, but this endeavour will make Bala Quila a dynamic and integral part of the community – not just another crumbling monument. There can be no greater tribute to history.

The local people I meet are enthusiastic in their support. Many of them are amateur historians, among whom the nattily dressed Himmat Singh stands out. His excellent, unaccented English indicates a public school education, as does his urging that I drop by later for a drink. Most people in small-town Rajasthan do not serve alcohol in their homes, and certainly not to women. I am intrigued, and accept.

Himmat is passionate about history. Dipping into an incongruous cloth shoulder bag, he produces a book on the history of Alwar published early this century. He delves into his bag again and produces a collection of photographs of the city before development occurred. He shows me photograph after photograph, comparing the old with the new. His enthusiasm is boundless and a little wearying.

He explains that Alwar's most recent dynasty only came into prominence in 1775. Its most prominent descendant was Raja Jai Singh, a controversial individual whose reputation ranges from the lurid to the fascinating.

'I am his grandson,' Himmat announces, to my astonishment. 'My father was his only son, but unfortunately he was illegitimate.'

Himmat's grandmother was Jai Singh's concubine, and the Maharaja not only recognised the son and daughter born of this liaison, but also granted his lady and her son a considerable estate. Since there was no legitimate heir, however, the succession passed elsewhere.

I retreat from the activity of the fort to a courtyard within the City Palace, backed by the Hawa Mahal, palace of breezes. The citizens of Alwar plan to bring the courtyard to life through musical evenings, to re-create the entertainments of the past. The pillared pavilion is open and airy, its stupendous views framed by slender pillars. Kites circle lazily far above the city swirling in the mist.

I wander off into the *zenana*, the wing where the royal women lived in strict seclusion. There are three floors of rooms around a central courtyard, each with fluid arches and long, cool arcades; the windows are small so as to keep out the heat and glare. It is a lovely structure but in urgent need of repair. The current inhabitants are bats and I can smell their acrid droppings.

My mind slips back to the past, when the *zenana* was alive

with feminine laughter, the rustle of brocaded *lehangas*, the tinkling of bangles and children's voices raised in play. Jewellers and cloth merchants would have come to sell their wares, bargaining with the ladies hidden behind reed curtains. Dancers and musicians would have thronged the court to entertain the secluded women; I can almost hear the jingling ankle bells, the thrumming of the tabla and the wail of the harmonium.

Manohar Kant Sharma joins me, and suggests a visit to Simla. I am nonplussed by his reference to the popular Himalayan resort. 'Wait and see,' he says, 'wait and see.'

Right in the middle of one of Alwar's many gardens, placed in an enormous sunken hollow, is an extraordinary domed, turreted and vaguely Gothic structure built of zinc. It is faintly reminiscent of a conservatory in Victorian England, but with a few Rajput embellishments.

'It's a fernery,' Manohar says, delighted at my surprise. 'It is so cool in there that it is named Simla.'

We descend a long flight of stairs, flanked by chutes that would once have been rushing cascades of water. I am beginning to get the general idea, but nothing prepares me for the staggering loveliness inside: there is greenery everywhere, trailing from baskets above my head, climbing up mock stone walls, creeping along the ground, bordering pathways and spilling over the flowerbeds, rockeries, grottoes and water gardens.

Manohar warns me to tread carefully as there is moss on the ground. Moss in arid Rajasthan! It is too much to take in. There are shades of green I have never imagined, from viridian and emerald to the palest lime, all artfully arranged in a gradated palette that seems natural but is beyond even nature's creativity. And everywhere there is rushing water, bubbling in channels along paved walkways, pausing in ponds covered in lotus leaves, tumbling over rocks and spilling over in waterfalls. 'Simla' may be quaint, it may be a Maharaja's whim, an anachronistic reflection in an oriental mirror, but for a Rajput escaping from the dry heat of Rajasthan it must have been wondrous.

Yuvrani Mahendra Kumari of Alwar, widow of the heir and mother of the next in line, was until recently the Member of Parliament for the Alwar constituency. I go to see her in a rather militant mood, as the party she represents, the Bharatiya Janata, has Hindu fundamentalist associations which are completely at odds with my fervent secular convictions. Her formidable name suggests a large, severe lady with hair tightly pulled back into a bun and a permanent disapproving frown.

My car is held up at the gate by some old retainers and new politicos, which adds to my negative attitude, and I resolve to barrage her with unpleasant questions. I am finally allowed to proceed to a comfortable bungalow, quite unlike the palace I had expected. The car is stopped again and I have to walk up the drive. By this time my ego is in overdrive and I am primed for battle.

Uniformed servants guide me through a marble foyer and into a bedroom. It is attractively appointed, with a large bed covered in a pleasing chutney-green fabric and a few old Regency chairs upholstered in matching green tapestry grouped around a small round table. Unlikely surroundings for a first meeting. I am trying to match this cool elegance with my mental picture of the lady when she quietly enters the room, wearing a white sari with a delicately scrolled green border. The edge of the sari is draped gracefully over her head, a mild affectation common among women from princely families and in keeping with her royal status. It frames a pert face with merry eyes that seem to struggle to be demure and proper.

We chat warily, each a little surprised by the other. I ask about her politics. 'Can we leave that subject alone?' she pleads. 'My interest is to work for the people, as the Alwar family has always done. I focus on building schools and colleges because I believe that without education, progress is impossible. Even the most comprehensive development schemes are ultimately meaningless without education. Education is empowerment.'

She smiles apologetically. 'Sorry, I got carried away, but this is my crusade.'

A magnificent black Newfoundland ambles into the room and places his large, shaggy head on her lap. 'This is Sultan,' she says. 'He is my first love. Animals are my real passion. I once had two pairs of lions, one from Africa and the other from Gir in Gujarat. How I loved them. I never allowed them to be caged, that's why our compound walls are so high, and they used to sleep in a room next to mine. But after my husband died the government took them away.'

We have passed the formal stage by now, and she asks me to

call her Kitten. It suits her, and recalls the fashion among the more anglicised princely families for English 'pet' names. They were often given by British governesses who could not cope with the longer syllables of Indian names.

Right up until 1991, when she went to the town hall to file her nomination as a candidate for the parliamentary elections, Kitten observed *purdah* in Alwar. Her appearance at the town hall was the first time the people of Alwar had seen the face of any royal woman from the ruling family.

'I never kept *purdah* at home,' she says ('home' was Bundi, where her father was the Maharaja). 'I also did not observe it in Delhi or Bombay, just in Alwar. And even here I only covered my face in the city.'

Although *purdah* was common all over India, it was fiercely enforced by the Rajputs. Many institutions developed around *purdah* but one of its strongest manifestations was in architecture. All palaces and *havelis* developed the women's section, the *zenana*, and various devices evolved to screen the women from view, including the delicate lattices through which the secluded ladies could watch the proceedings of the outside world. These intricately carved *jalis* also let in light and air, and were one of the most attractive characteristics of Rajput architecture.

I drop in as arranged for a drink at Himmat Singh's home that evening. We settle down in the drawing room, furnished attractively with solid old-fashioned sofas upholstered in rose velvet.

Himmat brings out a bottle of liquor distilled from saffron, a speciality from eastern Rajasthan.

The walls are painted with stylised representations of the sun, rays radiating from a central orb with big dark eyes and a curving Rajput moustache. The sun frescoes are a reminder that the Alwar family are Surya Vanshi Rajputs, claiming descent from the sun through the legendary god king Rama.

'In fact,' says Himmat, 'my grandfather believed he was an incarnation of Lord Rama.'

So obsessively did Jai Singh believe in his divine associations that he engaged scholars to study the scriptures to discover the exact form and dimensions of the crown worn by Rama, which he had copied and wore on all formal occasions.

'He was most eccentric,' Himmat says, and launches into a series of outrageous stories. Jai Singh's orthodox Hindu beliefs were so extreme that he believed that shaking hands with a non-Hindu would pollute him. So he always wore gloves: even when he was invited by King George and Queen Mary to Buckingham Palace for a reception.

'His veneration of the cow caused him to abhor leather,' Himmat tells me. So much so that the Hispano-Suizas he favoured, always ordered in threes and painted blue, the colour of Alwar, were upholstered in petit-point tapestry. 'They say that when he tired of the cars, he buried them,' Himmat laughs, with some embarrassment.

'British reports,' I remind him, 'described Jai Singh as villainous beyond belief and ascribed all kinds of vices to him.'

'The British! They were against him. Many of the stories they wrote about him are a pack of lies,' responds Himmat angrily, and then goes on to regale me with some of the more scurrilous anecdotes about his eccentric ancestor. One of the mildest describes his treatment of a favourite polo pony, which he beat mercilessly in the presence of a crowd of distinguished visitors before ordering that the pony be starved for two days. Another version has him douse it with petrol and burn it alive.

'They can't even get their stories straight,' he laughs with derision. 'He was one of only four princes in India with the courage and strength to hunt tiger on horseback with a spear. And yet they say he tied up old widows for tiger bait.'

Of Jai Singh's sexual preferences and orgies there are many whispered stories. One visiting ruler made a reference to the pretty boys Jai Singh always surrounded himself with. When he went to bed that night, the visitor found a nude young boy snuggled in the sheets. The boy produced a silk handkerchief from his bottom in proof of his cleanliness.

Himmat's wife Anapurna joins us. She is very quiet and I have to work hard to draw her into conversation. It turns out that she finds it a social embarrassment that she has no English. I tell her how ashamed and inadequate I feel that my Hindi is not as fluent and pure as hers – after all, Hindi is our language. I point out that many women I have met socially speak only Hindi.

'I still wouldn't know what to say to them, they would realise I am uneducated,' she whispers, twisting the end of her *odhni*.

But she slowly loosens up. 'The trouble is that I was in strict *purdah* till we were married,' she says. 'My life was very secluded and very uneventful. In fact I hardly ever left home and then only in a heavily curtained *purdah* car. It has had a bad effect on me, I can't bear to leave the house even now. I hate crowds, they frighten me. I don't even go out to do the household shopping, my husband or the boys do it for me.'

'She's lucky,' laughs Himmat, 'she doesn't have to bear the shock of rising prices.'

'But you mustn't think that I miss going out,' she says softly. 'I love my home and I am happy and fulfilled here. I never even go to parties with him,' she says, referring to her husband by a pronoun, for it would be disrespectful and dreadfully inappropriate for her to speak his name.

Himmat works in a bank during the week and is a motorcycle freak in his free time. He often takes time off to conduct motorcycle tours of Rajasthan, and he tells me with pride that he is the only Indian featured in the International Motorcycle Touring Directory.

'Riding on a motorcycle is quite an experience; you should try it some time,' he says.

That is exactly what I had been thinking, but I have a bad back and am afraid to take a long trip.

'We'll just go to Jai Sammand, one of the lakes that my grandfather built. The riding is smooth,' he assures me, 'no jerks or bumps. It's a short trip and you must experience the thrill of a bike at least once in your life.'

This is what I find so exciting about travelling: the unexpected encounters and diversions that make the journey unpredictable. We arrange to leave the next morning.

I dine with Manohar Kant and his wife that evening. Sarita is an interior decorator and has introduced a highly polished bullock cart full of green plants into their drawing room. Most of the other furniture is government issue, with a few carved occasional tables that she has designed. There are antimacassars over all the sofas and chairs. Sarita's training, especially her knowledge of old building techniques, has helped greatly in the restoration of the fort. She advises Manohar, who then guides his site engineers.

A visiting police officer has joined us for dinner. Yashwant Singh is a big, burly man with a sensitive face. His passions are history, bird watching and crime. We sit in the garden, which is cunningly lit with concealed lights that highlight a tree here, a shrub there. The air is gently fragrant with jasmine. And we talk about murder: *vair*, blood feuds, that are common in Rajasthan, especially among landowning classes. Most of the feuds are over land, water and women (in that order), or result from an insult, real or imagined. *Vair* sometimes simmers for generations, and when the victim's family is completely unsuspecting, revenge is taken in as bloody a manner as possible. Families have even been known to marry their daughter to a man whose grandfather's grandfather had incurred *vair*, and then with the girl's help, often her active participation, they murder her husband.

'*Vair* is most prevalent among the Rajputs and landed communities,' Yashwant says.

'And the others?' I ask. 'The tribes, the nomads, the Gypsies, the musicians?'

'They have no real possessions,' he smiles ironically, 'so there

39

is less to fight about.'

The system of collective justice is extremely well developed among the tribes and nomads. When there is a dispute, the entire village gathers. Both sides present their case, with much shouting and gesticulation, but even at its most vehement everyone remains seated. The deliberations last through the night, often for several days, until an acceptable and, as far as possible, unanimous decision is reached. Collective peer pressure then operates to ensure compliance.

The conversation shifts to crimes against women and, inevitably, *sati*. It was a particularly Rajput custom, symbolising ultimate wifely devotion and associated with Kshatriya notions of heroism and honour. When a man sacrificed his life on the battlefield, it was deemed appropriate that his equally brave Rajpootni wife should sacrifice her own.

The ghastly rite is named for the goddess Sati, wife of Shiva, who in protest against her father's dishonouring of her husband, leapt into the fire and died. Sati was 'rewarded' for this ultimate expression of loyalty by her subsequent rebirth as the goddess Parvati, and her marriage again to Shiva. Such myths endorsed the sanctity of a woman's supreme devotion to her husband, and were not restricted to Rajasthan but represented patriarchal traditions all over India.

'Increasingly, *sati* was practised by communities aspiring to higher status,' says Yashwant Singh. 'The custom was reinforced by the deep-seated belief that a woman should not outlive her husband, that her salvation lay in fulfilling the ultimate duty of a wife by accompanying him into the afterlife.'

The incentives were enormous. A *sati* would dwell in heaven for as many years as there were hairs on her body, and her act would absolve her of all sin. It would also guarantee salvation for her husband, and even her parents. But if she were not to become *sati*, she would be reborn as a woman repeatedly.

'Despite protestations to the contrary,' Yashwant Singh reminds me, 'few *satis* were purely voluntary. Coercion, blackmail and even physical force were used, or at the very least the spectre of an unhappy, dishonourable life.'

Sati was prohibited by law in the nineteenth century, but continued to be practised in secret. In September 1987, eighteen-year-old Roop Kanwar burnt to death on her husband's pyre at Deorala, in the Shekhavati area of Rajasthan. She loved her husband dearly and did not want to live without him, so she announced her decision to burn with him. The family was delighted: such a sacrifice would bring them great honour. The villagers too were supportive because they would benefit from the commerce engendered by the rite.

'The point,' says Yashwant Singh, 'was that Roop Kanwar grew up in a region that idolised *sati*. A huge temple at Jhunjhunu near her village commemorated a seventeenth-century *sati* who was worshipped as a goddess and believed to have miraculous powers. The girl was brainwashed from childhood. Worse, she was certainly given no chance to retract her decision. No-one cared that she was just a teenager, idealistic perhaps, indoctrinated certainly, but impetuous.'

The forthcoming event received much publicity, and on the appointed day a huge crowd gathered, including politicians from all the major political parties. Sword-wielding Rajputs encircled the area, threatening anyone who might dare to disrupt the sacred sacrifice of a woman who was already acclaimed a *devi*, or goddess. Roop Kanwar, dressed in the red and gold clothes she had worn as a bride, ascended the pyre. She sat down cross-legged and placed her husband's head in her lap. Her father's brother set fire to the wood. Today, a shrine has been erected to the girl goddess, and wives pray there for the wellbeing of their husbands.

I am consumed with anguish. Anguish at a society so obsessed with the past and conditioned by patriarchal values that it embraces such a barbaric practice. *Sati* is the most cruel illustration of the perceived dispensability of women and of its corollary, the overweening belief in male, and especially Rajput, superiority. The curse of Rajasthan.

Himmat arrives early the next morning, roaring down the hotel drive on his bike. As the jeans-wearing days of my distant youth are precluded by middle-aged spread, I've dressed for my motor-cycle experience in loose-fitting *salvar kameez*. I can't bring myself to swing my legs across the bike, so I sit primly and precariously side-saddle. Himmat kicks the bike into a steady roar that sends shivers down my spine.

'Hang on!' he calls cheerfully as we set off. To his credit and my enormous relief, he drives slowly and carefully, giving me time to adjust to the movement of the bike. I cling on grimly, desperately uncomfortable but afraid to move and scared out of my wits.

Slowly, very slowly, as we drive through the still-sleeping town, I gain a little confidence and wriggle on the pillion to make myself more comfortable. I begin to relax. Himmat revs the bike and we surge forward. My sensible ponytail is demolished, but I no longer care as the wind rushes through my hair. I feel joyous and carefree, eighteen again, but the odd bump helps me retain my sense of perspective and remember that although I might feel eighteen, I am closer to fifty and my back is nearer eighty.

The countryside rushes past, changing constantly. I would have thought it would be a blur but every detail stands out. The innumerable delicate shades of green in the fields marking the different stages of growth of the wheat. Fields of flowering mustard. The big, old trees that line the road. Farmers going out into their fields. An old man taking the cattle out to graze, his arms looped over the staff that rests comfortably across his shoulders. Chickens scratching in front of village houses. A dozing dog, black with white socks. Two black cows drawing water from a well, flanks gleaming in the sharp sun. Villages tend to be smaller here, and many houses appear to be empty: the families have moved to newly constructed homes in their fields.

The bike brings a sense of participation in the landscape, a greater immediacy: the wind, the sun, the speed, the noise all combine to make a potent high. I now understand why motorcycling is so addictive. You feel you are the only person in the world.

To my considerable alarm, Himmat turns off the main road

and onto a rutted and bumpy country lane. Just as I am getting accustomed to the bumps, we turn off onto a dirt track. Himmat doesn't help matters either.

'Watch out for dogs,' he yells above the roar and the wind. 'They tend to chase bikes and nip ankles.'

We stop eventually, to my great relief, at a large lake, sapphire blue and edged with white marble pavilions. It is wonderful to feel the earth beneath my feet again, and my legs tremble as though I can still feel the vibrations of the bike. We perch on the parapet wall, drinking cups of hot, sweet tea and watching the lake. A wind stirs the surface and the water ripples and swirls, wavelets glinting in the sun.

Himmat breaks into my reverie. 'Every Rajput king did three things during his rule. He built a temple for the gods, a palace for himself and a lake for his people.'

On my way to the Sariska Tiger Reserve, I take a new road along the outer perimeter of the sanctuary. The hills are like bare scalps and the foreground too is denuded, littered with stone and the remnants of marble quarries. Many mining concessions were owned by the rich and powerful and it took years of arbitration to close them down. The owners argued that Rajasthan is a poor state, and marble one of its few resources. Moreover, since the quarries were on the outskirts of the sanctuary, it was suggested that they weren't doing much damage – which was completely untrue, judging by the extreme deforestation and the devastation of habitat.

Among the activists involved in closing down the quarries was the Tarun Bharat Sangh, a voluntary organisation headquartered just outside the sanctuary. Rajender Singh, its prime mover, has dedicated his life to rural relief. We have met off and on over the years, sharing concerns and seeking advice, and I have decided on an impulse to visit him.

Rajender greets me with some surprise and considerable warmth. The *ashram*, a tiny green pocket surrounded by arid rocky soil, includes accommodation for a growing field staff as well as a residential facility for trainees and large halls for group discussions with local villagers. We talk sitting out on a paved area under the trees he has cosseted and coaxed to grow.

The organisation was established in 1975 by a group of young people committed to constructive social work. They had started off by working with pavement dwellers and the poorest of the urban poor in Jaipur, but had later realised that most of these people had migrated to the city because conditions in their villages were impossible. Their land was overworked, unproductive and unirrigated; any failure of the rains caused families to starve, and holdings were small, divided repeatedly among many sons. So it was inevitable that the focus of the group shifted to the rural poor.

'When we first came here in 1985,' Rajender recalls, 'the people were wary of us. Rumours circulated that we were procurers of young girls for the flesh trade. Suspicion was deep-rooted in these people, who had been exploited for generations.'

Gradually, over a year of discussion and interaction, they won the confidence and support of a few of the local people. The group came to believe that only the Gandhian model of village self-reliance could reverse the trend of rural decay.

'We first started talking to the women,' Rajender continues, 'trying to focus in on the region's primary problems, to identify areas where we could contribute. We found that it is the women who are the most effective catalysts for social change. They are the ones who bear the brunt of hardship.'

The women had spoken repeatedly about acute shortages of water, the primary cause of poverty in rural areas. The group decided to concentrate on creating small, earthen-walled dams in the villages. 'But we quickly understood,' Rajender adds, 'that unless the local people had some participation in the construction, maintenance would always be a problem. Although we raise seventy-five per cent of the resources to build these tanks, we insist that the villagers contribute the rest, either in cash or free labour.'

The role of trees and forests in conserving water was another important aspect of the scheme. 'We planted trees and initiated plantation projects on common village land,' Rajender explains. 'We supplied the saplings, but the village had to collectively plant and then protect the trees till they were beyond the reach of browsing goats and cattle.'

Rajender's group also worked towards the development of pastures, planting new kinds of grass that would better sustain and nourish livestock, and encouraged local people to protect the grasslands from overgrazing.

As a result of the group's efforts, people have begun to appreciate the link between the preservation of natural resources and their own welfare. We have a saying in Rajasthan that tiny drops of water eventually fill a big *matka* (in the rest of India, where water is not so scarce, people talk of tiny drops filling an ocean, not just a pot). It is with people like Rajender, not political or government organisations, that the future of India ultimately rests: people who do not pontificate in city drawing rooms, but go out to work among the poor, at considerable personal cost and deprivation.

Deep in the heart of the Sariska wildlife sanctuary are the crumbling walls of the Kankwari fort, once a strategic outpost and staging point where armies rested between long marches. Centuries of undergrowth encase its bastions and enormous, strapping trees grow out of the decaying masonry. A towering arched gateway leads to an overgrown and dusty forecourt.

'Wild animals often visit this isolated fort,' claims Ram Singh, the forest guard who has accompanied me on my visit. As if on cue there is a rustling in the undergrowth, and a dark shadow streaks out of the fort and disappears over a wall.

'Panther! Panther!' shouts Ram in high-pitched excitement. We rush through the undergrowth, scrambling under branches and dodging bushes, into a low, arched chamber that opens out onto the forecourt. It takes a few seconds for our eyes to adjust to the gloom and then we see a smear of blood on the ground, a long streak of browny red. The panther must have brought his kill here to eat it in peace and then rest up.

We labour up steep stairways to the first and second levels of the fort. Arched arcades open out on to a courtyard where there must have once been formal gardens, waterways and noisy fountains. The now-ruined palace would once have been hung with brocaded draperies and silken carpets; today, there are tiger droppings.

The views are spectacular from the uppermost level. Range after range of hills march into the distance, smothered in forest. Several stands of date palms testify to the presence of abundant subsurface water, for Ram tells me, 'They grow with their feet in water and their head in the sun.' I decide to spend the rest of the morning here, and settle down with my binoculars to watch deer coming to drink at the pool near the fort, water birds foraging for food and vultures riding the thermals.

Ram Singh returns with a villager in tow; both are carrying bulky packages. They lay out their contents on the parapet wall: *matkas* of thick fresh yogurt, large *rotis* of maize flour, a chutney of freshly ground garlic and red chillies and, to round it all off, large lumps of fresh, sweet *gur*. These are the staple foods of the average villager, and I devour them ravenously and with enormous relish.

Sariska is my favourite Project Tiger reserve. I spent many childhood holidays here with my parents, and after Ajit and I were married we came here often, with the children and on our own. So I have seen the sanctuary at many stages of its development and mine.

The sanctuary owes its existence, and the tiger its consequent preservation, to Maharaja Jai Singh, who developed the area as his hunting preserve. He received a lot of criticism for the roads and the palace he constructed within what is now the tiger reserve, but the controls that prohibited all but his personal guests from hunting there protected the wildlife. His interest in hunting ensured that cattle grazing was prohibited, since domestic livestock can communicate diseases which spread rapidly among deer and antelope.

Project Tiger was launched nationwide in the early 1970s, and has been one of the world's more successful conservation efforts. Today, India's tiger population is around two thousand, the world's highest. More importantly, the tiger has come to symbolise the health of the ecosystem, as the predator sits at the apex of the food chain.

When I was a child, long before Project Tiger was conceived, tigers were still baited at Sariska. A young buffalo was tied to a stake in an area a tiger was known to frequent. By dusk we were seated in a watchtower and I remember the thrill and the horror as the tiger made its kill, undisturbed by the spotlights to which it was well accustomed. The practice ceased, however, because it was felt that tigers were becoming too dependent on the bait. Plus the spotlighting and the tourists were said to be making the animals unafraid of humans and therefore easy prey to poachers.

It is late evening when I arrive at Sariska, just about the time tigers begin their evening prowl, and a good time for sightings. Ram Singh and I drive off the main road onto a track and scan the forest intently, watching for the smallest movement, the ever-so-slight quivering of a bush, the almost imperceptible flicking of ears or the gentle swishing of an impatient tail. There is the deliciously spine-chilling feeling that hidden feline eyes could be watching. Unlike the wide, open vistas of Africa, where animals are sighted from a distance, the Indian jungle is unpredictable, its dense undergrowth concealing many surprises. This is the jungle of my childhood, an unforgettable mix of dry deciduous forest, thorny shrubs, tall grasses and the musky smell of decaying leaves.

But this evening we have no luck. In my hotel room later that night, when sounds are magnified, a peacock calls plaintively and a chital deer barks, certain indications that a tiger or panther is near.

I'm back at the sanctuary by daybreak. Ram Singh has also heard the night sounds, and we creep forward into the forest with surging adrenaline. Ram suggests that we stop our jeep for a while, to listen to the jungle and look for circling vultures that could indicate a kill. It is strangely silent, and we speak in whispers.

Suddenly, the jungle erupts with a frenzy of alarm calls: monkeys hooping in agitation, birds chattering, deer barking and peacocks buzzing. It is a chain of sound that follows the path of the predator as each creature warns the other that the king of the jungle is on the move. Spotted deer browsing in a jungle clearing near us react to the calls; alert matriarchs, mindful of the danger, move their muzzles to face the direction of the wind and funnel their ears this way and that to catch the slightest sound. The deer are nervous, many stamping a forefoot in apprehension. And then there is complete, eerie silence, like the stillness that precedes a storm. Minutes tick away with agonising slowness, and the jungle gradually relaxes. The deer return to their browsing and we stretch and chat, laughing nervously.

Ram Singh knows the topography well and can identify the position of the tiger. 'He is crouched in a dry river bed just a few hundred metres away,' he says.

We drive hastily, eyes scanning the bush, and then Ram slows down and silently points. I look carefully in the direction he indicates and there, in the undergrowth, I see the tiger, his stripes merging with the dappled shadows. He is waiting to cross the road, making for the hillock on the other side. We wait and he waits. And then he tires of waiting – after all, what is there for a tiger to fear in his jungle? He crosses the road in a slow, measured stride, powerful muscles rippling. And we watch mesmerised, privileged spectators of the most splendid sight in the Indian jungle.

CHAPTER 2
JAIPUR

T HE DRIVE to Jaipur has jolted my body and jangled my mind. The traffic was impossible, backed up behind plodding camels, carts and tractors. To make matters worse, a dual carriageway is under construction and the road rutted beyond belief. I cut across town to Loharu House, where my politician friend Durru Loharu and his wife, Fauzia, have converted their sprawling mansion into a family hotel, which helps supplement the expenses of Durru's political life. It is my favourite retreat in Jaipur. I find relief here from the noise, traffic and hustle of the city I like least in Rajasthan.

Fauzia is busy at the popular kindergarten school she runs on the premises and I am welcomed by Durru, who is the Nawab of Loharu and a prominent Muslim leader. He is also a member of the Rajasthan State Legislative Assembly, where he represents our constituency, and one of the nicest people I know. Durru is the kind of person who is instinctively helpful, and as a result, his phone rings constantly and there is always a stream of people waiting to meet him on the verandah of Loharu House. He has many interesting ideas for my journey and gives me a lengthy list of friends to meet in Rajasthan. Most of the people don't seem to be very promising, however, as there is a homogeneous predictability about the 'upper class'; on the other hand, many of them do represent the state's feudal past.

I succumb to Durru's insistence that I meet a well-known astrologer, a Mr Chaturvedi. He is tall, silver-haired and distinguished, his fine features softened by time and compassion, and I take to him immediately. There is a sense of reassurance in his presence.

We settle down in the medium-sized room where he meets his patients ('clients' seems to be the wrong word, since he does not charge a paisa). The phone rings, and as he speaks into it I take in my surroundings. Blue walls with calendar cut-outs of various deities, a narrow sofa, matching chairs and a large desk. The room is typical of an average middle-class family anywhere in India.

Mr Chaturvedi turns to me apologetically. 'There was a problem about the marriage of a daughter. Her Venus is not very good and Venus is a causative factor in marriage. I decided to strengthen it by prescribing that she wear a diamond. But the family cannot afford such an expensive stone, so I suggested a cheap ring of diamond chips.'

Mr Chaturvedi recently retired from the Indian Railways after a forty-year tenure. He now devotes his life to using a combination of astrology and gemology to help people in distress. 'Astrology,' he says, 'is a perfect science. The only problem, mind you, is that sometimes I'm given the wrong birth time and that causes difficulties.'

Medical gemology is his forte, but as it is not a well-known field of study, patients resort to it only when all other cures have failed. 'It is important that a person come to me at the appropriate time,' he continues. 'If the problem is too deep-seated it is often difficult to resolve. Different stones affect different parts of the body. For problems in the brain, cat's-eye is effective. Sapphire is most helpful for the lower back and the legs, in fact for most difficulties with the bones. Gomed, a stone similar to a garnet, alleviates heart problems. Diamonds and pearls are associated with peace of mind; they win you friends and bring prosperity and peace, so naturally these are popular stones.'

Similarly, each planet rules a particular part of the body: Saturn, for example, controls the head and the backbone. Mr Chaturvedi combines the appropriate stone for the affected part of the body with the day ruled by the planet that governs the complaint, and that determines when the stone should be worn. Depending on the patient's horoscope, other stones are also prescribed.

I look at him unconvinced. 'But there is a rationale behind gemology,' he insists. 'For thousands upon thousands of years, a particular piece of stone has received the sun in a manner regulated by the formation of the mother rock. The sun acts on the materials within each stone, whether it be a diamond, sapphire or ruby, and each absorbs certain rays in a certain way. Thus, a gem is really a form of compacted energy, which when worn next to the skin, the most sensitive part of the body, counteracts the deficiencies that cause illness.'

Just as I am beginning to get it all straight, he complicates the issue further. 'The fingers are also related to different planets, so the particular finger on which the prescribed ring is worn is also important.'

While I try to figure this out, Mr Chaturvedi interjects, 'Take yourself for example. You should wear a pure white diamond on the ring finger of your left hand. You must also wear a pearl on the small finger of that hand. The pearl should be worn on a Monday, the diamond on a Friday.'

'I have told you nothing about myself,' I protest, 'not even my date of birth. How can you prescribe for me?'

'Offhand I'd say you were born in early August, probably on a Friday.'

He is absolutely correct, but then a skilled astrologer would easily be able to recognise sun-sign traits.

'You like white flowers that are lightly scented,' he continues, clearly enjoying himself. 'Your favourite is probably the tuberose.'

This time I am less sceptical. I think of the white garden we have planned at Patan and our ongoing search for plants with white blossoms. I think also of the large numbers of tuberoses I have persuaded Ajit to plant, despite his strong antipathy to seasonal flowers.

While we have been talking, several people have come into the room. Each person touches Mr Chaturvedi's feet respectfully, leaves a small offering of fruit on his desk and sits down to wait. When I realise that anyone can witness his consultations, I decide to stay a while and listen.

55

The first patient is a mason, a thin, stringy man, wearing his very best sparkling-white *dhoti* and a blue shirt. He has been out of work for a long time, and he does not have a horoscope. Mr Chaturvedi tells him to recite a particular mantra five times every Tuesday.

After the man has left he explains to me, very quietly, 'I prescribe mantras because sound vibrations also have strong therapeutic qualities. They ward off negative planetary influences and also help strengthen resolve.'

Another man has a problem with his heart. He complains of breathlessness and a heaviness in his arms. 'In my dreams I often see wolves,' he says, worry creasing his forehead, 'always I am chasing wolves.'

'Dark wolves?' Mr Chaturvedi asks.

'Yes, yes,' the patient replies with some surprise, 'they're not the usual grey-brown of wolves, but almost black.'

The man is given detailed instructions on the kind and weight of the stone he should wear, the metal of the setting, and the finger and day on which the ring should be worn.

A couple are next. The man has an air of complete hopelessness, while the woman wears a pugnacious expression. Mr Chaturvedi speaks to them at length, and I gather from snippets of the conversation that their child has died. He prescribes a cat's-eye.

'You must be strong,' he tells the bereaved couple, and instructs them to recite a mantra and light scent sticks before an image of Hanuman – the deity known as the monkey god – worshipping at the same time and same place every day.

As they leave, they place a bunch of bananas in a pink plastic bag on the desk. Mr Chaturvedi addresses me in a quiet aside. 'This couple have a major problem with their karma. What happens is this. People you have caused trouble to in a previous life will be associated with you again in this life, and will visit the same sorrow on you that you caused them. The person could be reborn as your child, your husband, your boss or in some other capacity. It is important to understand that we have contributed in some measure to our current unhappiness.'

I tell him that I subscribe to the snuffed-candle theory, that I believe in the present, in this one life.

'A blind child born to healthy parents, how do you account for it?' he asks. 'Karma. Two men are born on the same day, at the same time: one achieves success, the other does not. Why? Karma. People you have harmed in a previous life must all take their revenge in this one. And they will continue to take their revenge for seven generations.'

Another manifestation of past lives, according to Mr Chaturvedi, is the particular attraction you feel for some people as soon as you meet them. This is because your soul and theirs have already met. 'There are no coincidences,' he insists, 'everything that happens is meant to happen.'

A middle-aged lady has entered the room. The clusters of diamonds twinkling in her ears indicate that she is clearly more affluent than most other people here. She tentatively hands Mr Chaturvedi a horoscope. He looks up after studying the chart. 'A strong-willed girl, there is some danger of love marriage here.'

The lady sighs and takes out another horoscope from the

plastic bag full of papers that she is carrying. 'This is the horoscope of the boy she has fallen in love with. They met at college. It is a most unsuitable match: he is of the wrong caste and is not financially in the same class as us. What will people say?' she says, twisting the end of her sari.

Mr Chaturvedi studies the new chart and compares it with that of the lady's daughter. 'The horoscopes match,' he tells her. 'It will be a good marriage, a very happy one.'

'But what will people say? They will think there is something wrong with our family that we have not been able to get a better boy. There will be a lot of talk. And I have one more daughter and two sons to marry. This could affect their chances of finding good matches.'

'Love marriage is not such a bad thing,' Mr Chaturvedi says in a sympathetic voice.

The only way to attempt an understanding of Jaipur and its Kachhwaha Rajput rulers is to start at Amber, built soon after the dynasty came to power in the region. The tedious drive through heavy traffic to the old capital is relieved by the beauty of Jaipur's buildings, their pink exteriors contrasting with the white borders and floral motifs that define latticed windows and decorate balconies, kiosks and pavilions.

The distinctive colour of Jaipur's buildings has been described as 'deep oleander pink' and 'crushed strawberry'. It was thought to have been applied to the city as part of the clean-up carried out in anticipation of the 1876 visit of Albert, Prince of Wales (later Edward VII). However, a miniature painted over a hundred years before the royal visit shows the City Palace and the buildings in its vicinity painted pink. The choice of colour was probably influenced by the red sandstone favoured by the Moghuls, but sandstone was expensive and stone buildings took a long time to construct, so Jaipur's buildings were simply washed with a mixture of lime and red earth.

I am accompanied by Raj Singh, a guide from the department of tourism, who is the quintessential Rajput with his well-tended moustache and bold eyes. 'My ancestors fought with the Maharajas of Jaipur,' he tells me. 'I was born and brought up here.'

He has a passion for history, which is why he decided to take up 'guiding'. We talk about the history of the Kachhwahas, of Raja Bhar Mal of Amber and the controversy he stirred up when he cemented an alliance with the Moghul emperor Akbar by giving him his daughter in marriage in 1556.

Raj Singh voices his indignation. 'That was almost thirty years after the combined armies of the Rajputs were soundly defeated by Babur, Akbar's grandfather. If all the Rajputs together could not hold out against the Moghuls, how could they expect the Kachhwahas to do so? Especially as Amber was the kingdom closest to Delhi.'

Bhar Mal's was a practical decision, taken to ensure the safety of the state and its future prosperity. Although other Rajput rulers soon followed suit, they were all loud in their condemnation of the Kachhwahas for being the first to give in.

Kachhwaha honour vindicated, we are now able to take in the

59

scenery. Fort walls snake along the contours of the surrounding hills, culminating in Jaigarh fort, Amber's main defence. The Kachhwahas' fabled treasure is said to be hidden here, a priceless collection of gems and jewels, one of the richest hoards in the country. The treasure disappeared sometime between the 1940s, when the previous Maharaja of Jaipur displayed a jewelled bird, and 1977, when income-tax officers searched the fort and grounds with metal detectors, but found nothing. Jaipur has buzzed with speculation ever since.

We pass though a gorge and come upon Amber glowing in the afternoon sun. Twenty-eight kings ruled from here for over six centuries. The fort clings to a hillside and its stern façade is relieved by frivolous cupolas, minarets and domes, all mirrored in the still waters of the nearby lake.

A sign near the base of the fort makes me smile: 'Elephant Complaints Here'. Surely this must be the only such sign in the world. Complainants are directed to the tourist office which monitors the sixty elephants that carry visitors up to the fort. I locate the next available elephant and clamber onto its *howdah*. A family of three from Calcutta are already 'on board' and I make up the necessary party of four. The great beast – her name, I discover, is Bubblie, an Indian equivalent of Poppet – lurches to her feet and we are off. The perspective is different from this height, and Amber appears less formidable.

We lumber up a narrow road enclosed by high walls, through gate after gate. Since I am seated closest to the head of the elephant, I fall into conversation with its mahout. He tells me that his family have been mahouts for so many generations that he has lost count.

'My father, may Allah bless him, was the personal mahout of Maharaja Man Singh. The Maharaja would never sit behind any other.'

'And your children,' I ask, 'will they also be mahouts?'

'For the lifetime of our remaining three elephants only. There is no joy left in this profession. Even my father, Allah rest his soul, told me that respect for elephants has reduced. Now that there are cars, he said to me, make your children learn some other trade. So some became car mechanics, others jewellers, printers. My father knew a lot about remedies for elephants. The biggest problems are wind and colds.'

The consequences of an elephant with a wind problem are too horrific to imagine – and as for an elephant with a runny nose . . . !

In the old days, there were ninety-nine elephants in the palace stables; the hundredth was always given away to someone the Maharaja wanted to ruin, as the cost of feeding an elephant would ensure his downfall. Today, even the Maharaja has none.

The mahout tells me of the Jaipur Maharajas' enormous elephant-drawn chariot, so tall that its 'garage' outside the City Palace is almost two storeys high. Some years ago, the Maharaja decided to use it on a ceremonial occasion. The chariot was pulled out with a tractor and the elephants were harnessed to it. 'But our undernourished animals were too weak to draw it.'

By this time we have approached the last gate and I get an elephant's-eye view of Amber's splendid palaces, most of which were built during the reign of Maharaja Man Singh I, who ruled from 1590 to 1614. One of the highest-ranking nobles of the Moghul court and one of its most prominent generals, Man Singh was a connoisseur of the arts. Since the agricultural potential of Jaipur, and most of Rajasthan, was limited by lack of water, he made Amber a major centre of the arts by bringing skilled artisans from all over the country to his city. Thus, he provided the first impetus for the crafting of objects of both utility and great beauty, later closely associated with Jaipur.

I am reunited with my guide, Raj Singh, and we enter the fort, ascending many stairs and passing through long corridors to reach the old *zenana*. Maharaja Man Singh's twelve queens each had separate quarters, each with a private staircase to the royal bedchamber. 'The separate apartments were essential,' says Raj Singh, 'because there were jealousies among the queens and the danger of one murdering another's child.'

Multiple marriages were the norm in those days, a strategic ploy to create alliances with as many powerful kingdoms as possible. The fact that women were used in the process is dismissed as a matter of tradition. 'Tradition' is a powerful word among Rajputs; it explains away everything. The more wives there were, the better the chance of begetting a legitimate male heir. Yet several Rajas burnt out on opium and their many concubines and mistresses, and consequently found it necessary to adopt a successor.

'One thing I have observed,' Raj Singh remarks, 'is that both Rajas and policemen often do not have an heir. I think it has something to do with bad karma.'

We move on through a procession of gilded and decorated

chambers, and I think I have seen all the fort has to offer, when I reach the famous Sheesh Mahal, the palace of mirrors, the most outrageously ostentatious of them all.

'The glass was blown into round balls,' Raj Singh tells me, 'and while it was still hot, mercury was poured in to cover the concave interiors. The balls were then broken and the pieces shaped to be inset.'

A group of young girls walk past, and I watch the bright colours of their clothes reflected many thousands of times. In the mosaic at my feet, replicated in stone, are flowers. I am engrossed in the turn of a leaf, the wrinkling of a petal as if blown by a breath of air.

'Look carefully,' Raj Singh urges, 'and you will find multiple forms.' He shows me a snake, a scorpion, a fish and an elephant's trunk, all within a single flower.

I decide to visit Bridgette, a friend of Fauzia's who lives just beyond Amber. A French woman married to a Rajput, she is reputed to create the finest block printing in Jaipur.

Bridgette's home and workplace, inspired by local *haveli* architecture, is built around a central courtyard. It has honey-col-oured stone walls and pillars, carved door frames of red sandstone and floors that are harlequined in ochres and greys.

We meet with reservations on both sides: Bridgette because she is wary of publicity, me because I am tired of seeing the same old prints from the Jaipur region ever since block printing by hand became fashionable again about thirty years ago.

'I came to India thanks to the Ayatollah Khomeini,' Bridgette laughs. She was on her way to Iran to study Persian miniatures when the American hostage crisis started, so she came to Rajasthan instead. Bridgette discovered that the intricate floral patterns of Rajput miniature paintings could be replicated on hand-printed fabrics. Her work is detailed and innovative, emulating the delicate definition of Moghul textiles. Such excellence was achieved in the old days because production was not based on demand. Bridgette follows the same course: 'I work on a tiny scale,' she says, 'producing only minute quantities.'

In her opinion, the main problem that afflicts the production of handcrafted goods in Rajasthan is the lack of innovative design. She speaks about the crucial role of the designer as intermediary between craftsperson and consumer, believing it to be the only realistic and sustainable bridge between Jaipur's heritage and the future.

Later, we walk through Bridgette's garden to an orchard of lemon and pomegranate trees, interspersed with patches of bright flowers. She tells me about the family traditions that once nurtured crafts. The larger homes included permanent workshops and ateliers for the artists who painted the members of the family and scenes from their lives. 'Photography did away with all that,' she says.

We discuss the aesthetics of miniature painting, which I have never properly understood. Bridgette has an unusual theory to explain the popularity of the form. 'Indians have meticulous minds. For example, there is no more meticulous grammar than Sanskrit. Indian life is governed by detail, detail, detail,' she laughs, pausing to inhale the sharp fragrance of a lemon flower. 'Look at the words that define relationships. Take the word "aunt" for instance. In India there are so many different categories of aunts, and each requires a different term. There is a word for your mother's sister, father's sister, mother's brother's wife, father's brother's wife. And within each classification there are different words for the eldest and the youngest. The same attitude permeates every relationship – they are all minutely categorised.'

I ask her opinion, as a painter, about the impulse for decoration in Rajasthan: the joyous, uncontrolled revelling in colour and form, its exuberance and extravagance unmatched in any other part of India. We both discount the usual explanation of a reaction against the drabness of Rajasthani landscapes.

Bridgette thinks for a while. 'There is a definite preference for the colourful and shiny, an almost childlike enjoyment. One of the things I love about living in Rajasthan is that I can wear as much jewellery as I like and get away with it. Perhaps it's a manifestation of my continuing childhood. I can wear the kind of stuff that would make me dreadfully overdressed in most other places. I went to a wedding the other day,' she says, her eyes shining, 'just for the fun of dressing up.'

Scientific inquiry is the last thing one associates with Rajasthan, yet it was a field of study which held great interest for Maharaja Jai Singh. When he was born in 1688 at Amber, court astrologers predicted that he would be the brightest star of the Kachhwaha dynasty. They were not far wrong: he charted the galaxy at the Jantar Mantar, the house of instruments, said to be the world's largest and best preserved open-air observatory.

Jai Singh studied Hindu, Muslim and European works on astronomy and reached the conclusion that existing calculations of the positions of the planets and stars were inaccurate. Like Muslim astronomers of his day, he believed that the only barrier to accurate observation was the limitation of the instruments available, so he decided to eliminate error by building enormous, perfectly stable devices made of stone and lime. By 1724 Jai Singh had completed the first observatory at Delhi, but the biggest and most elaborate one, the Jantar Mantar, was established in the City Palace at Jaipur, the new capital built by and named for him.

I am intrigued by Jai Singh, a conscientious if somewhat out-of-step citizen of the age of enlightenment, tragically isolated from contemporary developments in the West. Had it been otherwise, his power and wealth might have enabled him to alter the whole direction of scientific thought in India. Newton's *Principia* had been written around the time of his birth, and in 1705 Halley had predicted the return of the comet, but Jai Singh remained unaware of these developments. Although his observatory at Jaipur was built forty years after Greenwich, and over a hundred after the invention of the telescope, his achievements relied on the naked eye and thus remain all the more remarkable.

At the *zenana* in the City Palace, I speak to Jadu Singh, the guard on duty. 'Part of the *zenana* is still inhabited,' he informs me. 'The present Maharaja's grandfather had many ladies in his harem, and although they are dead, some of their personal attendants, entertainers and descendants still live here.'

Curiously, their expenses are met by the Governor of Rajasthan, for when the government took over the assets of Jaipur State in 1952, the Maharaja told the government, 'Since you are taking my assets, it's only fair that you also take my liabilities.'

About a decade ago, perhaps more, these women were told that they could leave the *zenana* if they wished; they each received a handsome financial settlement and arrangements were made for them to go back to their villages. Within a couple of weeks they were all back. After a lifetime in seclusion, the outside world was too much for them.

Until recently the entrance to the *zenana* was guarded by a eunuch. 'Nadir Babaji, that was his name. He died just a couple of years ago.'

I ask if Nadir Baba was a Rajput. Jadu is indignant. 'Eunuchs were never Rajputs!' Apparently they were usually from the lower castes, people so poor that the possible wealth that could be accumulated from castration made the dreadful mutilation an acceptable alternative to poverty. Eunuchs controlled the *zenana* and were extremely powerful. It was mandatory, within reasonable limits and within the bounds of royal preference, for the Maharaja to visit each of his ladies from time to time and the rotation was dictated by the head eunuch. Since the eunuch could always steer the Raja away from a particular woman by claiming that she was 'indisposed', his favour was courted by all the women in the *zenana*.

'Several eunuchs accumulated huge estates,' says Jadu, enjoying the gossip, 'but they all spent their money lavishly on drink, sex, rich clothes and jewellery.'

Life in the *zenana* had many material comforts but also many restrictions. 'No whole things were allowed into the harem,' Jadu Singh says with some delicacy. I do not understand and he attempts to explain, coughing frequently to hide his embarrassment. 'Well, you know, carrots, cucumbers, horseradish – all these things were cut up before they were sent into the *zenana* kitchens.'

He chews his *paan* reflectively and tells another story closer in time. A few years ago the current Maharani wished to make a gift to one of the old ladies in the *zenana*, and after some deliberation decided that she might enjoy a transistor radio. A couple of months passed and it was felt that the batteries had probably run low, so an official was sent in to deliver some new ones. Naturally, the conventions were observed and the lady spoke with him through a screen.

'We discovered,' says Jadu Singh, 'that she had no idea what this strange object was. But since it was a gift from the Maharani it was worthy of veneration, so she lit scent sticks before the radio and offered flowers to it every morning.'

The official explained the function of the object, and turned on the set to some Indian film music. The lady ran away screaming in fear.

Fauzia, Durru and I sit on the deep verandah of Loharu House, looking out over the garden and chatting. Durru and I fall into a conversation we have often had about problems in the Patan region. Of particular concern to all of us is the conversion of agricultural land to industrial use, a wanton waste of a non-renewable resource.

'In a state like ours,' Durru says with some anger, 'it is essential to conserve every centimetre of productive land, instead of turning it into blocks of concrete.'

Industry, which we agree is an important activity, should be relocated on degraded land with little agricultural value. There is also the question of the future of farmers who have sold their land. The vast sums of money they receive are simply beyond their comprehension, and ancestral assets that have sustained families for generations are squandered within a couple of years. Durru is working towards introducing legislation in Rajasthan to prevent this conversion of land into cash, for the problem is not limited to the Patan area but has spread across the state.

As a Muslim, Durru is also deeply concerned about the situation of Muslims in Rajasthan, as the state is dominated by the right-wing Bharatiya Janata Party, which is committed to Hindu revivalism. I bring up the historical antipathy of the Rajputs towards Muslim rulers, whom they regarded as 'foreign' invaders.

'The first Muslim kingdom,' Fauzia reminds me, 'was established at Delhi by the end of the twelfth century. Within a few decades they began to consider India as their home, not as a place to plunder and leave. And under the Moghuls, of course, after

69

Akbar's policy of marrying Hindu women, all subsequent emperors had Rajput blood.'

The majority of Rajasthan's four and a half million Muslims are descended from these kings, their nobles and staff, all of whom also intermarried. Some, like Durru's family, were rulers of independent states, others were large landowners, and many of the important generals in Rajput kingdoms were also Muslim. There were large rural Muslim communities too, and many thousands of artisans who lived in harmony with their Hindu neighbours, sharing rituals and social customs.

Everything began to change in the years that preceded Independence and Partition in 1947, when the subcontinent was torn apart on the premise that the Muslim and Hindu communities, who had lived together for centuries and who were of the same blood and race, were two separate peoples. Religious hysteria was whipped up among both communities by politicians whose only consideration was power. People went mad on both sides and committed unbelievable atrocities. Millions of Muslims migrated to Pakistan and an equal number of Hindus moved to India, butchering each other in passing. Today, fifty years later, only some of the wounds have healed, and people from both communities have become the unwilling victims of a tug of war between fundamentalists.

We speak of the many problems that beset the Muslim minority, a community that has been treated as a vote bank and increasingly isolated. 'According to the census in 1991,' says Durru, 'there are over four million Muslims in Rajasthan. But there are only two Rajasthani Muslims in the Indian Administrative Service, and none in the Indian Police. And there is not a single Muslim Member of Parliament from Rajasthan.'

These horrifying figures indicate the lower level of education among the state's Muslims, and also a subtle discrimination. 'But it will pass,' says Durru, 'I am confident. Remember that India has one of the world's largest Muslim populations, and that the green in our national flag represents Islam.'

The conversation with Fauzia and Durru reminds me of a visit I made some years ago to Jhunjhunu in the Shekhavati region. I travelled to the town's Muslim quarter to visit a specialist in *unani* medicine. Driving through the area's narrow streets, I felt ill at ease, an outsider. The neighbourhood appeared to be fortified, largely because of the buildings' uniformly high walls, and every single sign was in Urdu. I was very aware that I was in the middle of an ethnic enclave built for protection against the hostile Hindu world, and although I was not a Hindu, I was not a Muslim either.

We eventually found our destination, but the doctor was not at home. His family, however, invited me into their home, and we chatted over a cup of tea. I could hear children's voices raised in song and I asked where the singing was coming from.

'We run a girl's school on our rooftop,' Osman, the doctor's son, explained. 'Most conventional Muslim families do not send their girls to school. You can say this is a *purdah* school.'

Osman told me that the children were reciting the Koran in Arabic. This would be followed by a study of the scripture, also in Arabic, and lessons in Urdu.

'What about Hindi?' I asked. 'Will they learn Hindi?'

'What would they do with Hindi? They don't even leave the house without an escort.'

'Can you sing the Jana Gana Mana?' I asked the girls, referring to the Indian national anthem. None of them knew what I was talking about. It struck me that these children were growing up as foreigners in their own state, unable even to speak the language of the majority.

'You must remember that the Koran is in Arabic,' was Osman's response. 'So are most of the prayers. Arabic is very much a living language.'

'In the Arab world, yes; but certainly not in India. These children may be able to recite the entire Koran and say their prayers, but they do not understand what they are saying. Even if they are taught the meaning of the prayer, it is impossible for them to fully comprehend the meaning, let alone the nuances.'

I raised the possibility of the children learning a translation of the Koran – a Hindi translation. 'There are difficulties in translation,' Osman replied. 'First of all there is the importance of making an exact translation that doesn't dilute or change meaning. Also, much of the power of recitation comes from the power inherent in combinations of sound, from the state of sanctity it induces, like a mantra. The sound patterns are as important as the words.'

I could see his point, yet the enormity of the problem made me feel helpless. How to bridge the chasm that so tragically isolates India's Muslims?

Among Durru's many visitors one seems vaguely familiar. She

turns out to be Srilata, an old friend from my days in Delhi, whom I last saw about thirty years ago. She was always a bit of a rebel, and created a considerable stir in India's conservative 1960s by deciding to go to the National School of Drama instead of college. She taught there for several years, and many of the big names in Indian cinema were once her students. I lost touch with Srilata around this time and heard that she was doing crazy things: she had joined the Communist Party for one, and gone off into the wilds of Rajasthan to work with tribal peoples. It all sounded typically Srilata, but for years I had wanted to understand what motivated her.

We go into a huddle to catch up. Srilata is now a member of the Marxist–Leninist Communist Party, a splinter group formed to create more democracy within the Party. It had all started off with some social work among farm labourers on the outskirts of New Delhi, an area of up-market weekend farms and country homes. 'Owned by people like us, or rather by people who are friends of our parents.'

Srilata discovered that these landowners were paying their labourers way below the stipulated minimum wage. 'I was disgusted with our kind of people. It's like a club: we all speak the same language, go to the same schools, are members of the same organisations. We make the rules, which are weighted in our favour.'

Srilata spearheaded a group of agitators and ended up in jail. 'I met prostitutes, petty thieves and many other female criminals,' she says, 'and I discovered that they were all happy to be in prison. It represented shelter, food and rest. That really blew my mind. I decided that I would devote the rest of my life to changing the system.'

After Srilata joined the Party she decided to move to the tribal belt of south-western Rajasthan, to work among the poorest and most deprived people in the country. Generations of Rajput settlers had evicted these people from their lands and pushed them into the hills, where they lived on the edge of starvation, farming degraded, low-yielding land.

'That was the beginning of my transition from a butterfly to a caterpillar. I was urban, westernised and I knew nothing. I had to learn to understand how eighty per cent of our people lived. How did all those things we had read about, like feudalism and poverty, actually affect their lives?'

She decided that in order to understand, she had to live among the people, to live as they did. 'I had never cooked on a wood fire, I had never bathed in a stream with all my clothes on, I had never gone into the bushes to relieve myself, nor finished the walls and floor of a mud hut with cow dung. I didn't even know how to grind my own maize.'

The people later told her that they used to laugh at her. 'I didn't know that cooking on a wood fire blackened my hands,' she says, laughing herself, 'and since I didn't have a mirror, I never knew that I always had black streaks across my face. It was an incredible learning experience, an enormous challenge. A process of coming to terms with myself, my snottiness and my conditioning, and learning to cope with it.'

'What were you really trying to achieve?' I ask.

'Well, five per cent of India takes eighty per cent of the

nation's resources. That includes jobs. We are not a democracy until this evens out.'

'So?'

'So I want to make people aware, make them fight for their rightful share.'

And the results?

'We'll see them in the next generation maybe, perhaps the one after that, or even two hundred years from now. But change has begun.'

CHAPTER 3
AJMER

I T IS dark when we leave Jaipur for Ajmer, and the tedium of the bumper-to-bumper traffic is aggravated by trucks driving with their headlights on full beam. We are taking the main highway linking Rajasthan with Delhi and Bombay, and there is a sense that the nation is on the move with a roaring, anarchic vitality.

I have long looked forward to visiting Ajmer, as its history had far-reaching consequences for the rest of Rajasthan. One of the last great Hindu empires was governed from Ajmer until it was extinguished in the late twelfth century by the invader Muhammad Ghori; the defeated king, Prithviraj Chauhan, has always been one of my favourite historical characters. Ajmer is situated in the centre of Rajasthan and was often the key to the region's conquest: several Moghul emperors used it as a base for campaigns further south and west, and it later became a strategic garrison from which the British controlled Rajputana.

I doze for a while and waken close to Ajmer. All I can see of its environs is the uneven outline of encircling hills, natural defences that have protected the city from destructive winds and invading armies.

I am a little unfocused the next morning and dither about where to start my visit. Apparently, my car can't make it up the steep incline to Taragarh, the citadel of Prithviraj Chauhan, but to go directly to the other monuments, largely of the Moghul period, would be to start in the middle of Ajmer's past. I feel the need to go back to the city's beginnings, and I share my dilemma with a young tourist officer, who has an unusual idea. 'Why don't you visit the puppeteers?' he suggests. 'They perform an entire episode about Prithviraj Chauhan.'

It seems an excellent opportunity to combine an exploration into the art of puppetry, the most ancient form of theatre and a favourite entertainment in Rajasthan, with a dramatised introduction to history. The officer directs me to the edge of the town, where a few families of puppeteers have settled in some mud huts. The forecourts are covered in a fine mixture of cow dung and clay, which forms an even surface that is easy to sweep.

A tall, slim man in his mid-thirties greets me with a politeness that hides his curiosity. Gulab Singh has the mobile eyes and dramatic gestures of an actor. I explain that I would like to see a puppet show on the story of Prithviraj Chauhan. 'Let's talk about it over a cup of tea,' he suggests.

Gulab Singh explains that the puppets mean a great deal to his family: 'They are our bread and butter, so we treat them with reverence.' An old puppet, I discover, is never discarded but kept in the home like an honoured but aging relative.

'In the past our puppets were much simpler, but innovations

were introduced over the centuries so that today the puppets are much more complicated. See,' he says, holding up a male marionette with a brightly painted wooden face, large, accentuated eyes and sharply defined features. Its body of stuffed cloth is draped with a spangled robe, and a turban with a glittering plume rests on its head. 'This is a traditional puppet, one of the Rajas. He has only two strings.'

He delves into a cloth bag and produces a female puppet with similarly sharp features, shining jewellery and a red and gold *lehanga* and *odhni*. 'Now this is one of the new kind. A courtesan. She has six threads because we must be able to make her move effectively.' He manipulates the threads and the lady dances, moving her hands and feet, hips undulating suggestively. Gulab Singh beams with pride. 'See, she can bend both backwards and forwards. We use her a lot for entertainment sequences. After all, whenever kings gathered they were entertained by dancing girls.'

Gulab Singh warms to his subject and produces four puppets that are attached by strings to a crossbar, and so can be manipulated together. 'These are even newer developments, they are our male dancers who perform the *ger*.' He pulls the strings and the dancers leap into action, gyrating and striking the sticks in their hands against those of their partners. 'You see, as other forms of entertainment developed, radio, TV and so on, we had to make our shows more appealing.'

More complex puppets were developed with greater dramatic and visual potential, but the new puppets still have the stylised, brightly painted faces and prominent eyes of the older ones, features which were developed over the centuries to provide better visibility on dimly lit stages.

'This is our newest addition,' Gulab Singh tells me, displaying a smiling character with a turban. 'This is the magician, a comic character with tremendous capability for movement. His speciality is that he can take off his head, bounce it in the air or balance it on his feet. Our audiences love this fellow. We use these characters to lighten the mood, otherwise people get bored. The laughter makes it easier for us to communicate the messages of chivalry and bravery that it is our *dharma* to perpetuate.'

Puppeteers require many skills: carving the puppets, painting their faces, creating clothes and ornaments. Then they must know the many traditional stories based on the heroic legends of Rajasthan, none of which are written down, but which are passed from generation to generation. They must also be showmen, with a flair for dramatic delivery, and, of course, they must be able to manipulate the strings.

Unlike many art forms that have become ossified, pallid imitations of previous performance patterns without relevance or vitality, puppetry is alive and well. The puppeteers have responded to changing needs with resourcefulness and creativity, and I look forward to the performance of the Prithviraj Chauhan story, planned for the following evening.

Back at the tourist office, young Hemant Sharma, who has made it his business to study the history of Ajmer, agrees to show me around. He has just returned from a 'party' at Pushkar.

'Some British tourists wanted to organise a disco party with disc jockeys and all. I helped hire the equipment locally and they had their own music. I had never seen a disc jockey work, neither had I been to a disco, so I decided I must have this experience.'

He left the party at six in the morning and it was still in full swing. I am interested in the aspects of culture shock, but Hemant is far too nice to be judgmental. He is also most discreet. 'It was quite an experience,' he keeps repeating, running his hands through his hair.

Our first stop is deep in the old city, at the famous tomb of the twelfth-century Sufi mystic from Persia, Hazrat Khwaja Muin-ud-din Chishti, who settled in Ajmer. A direct descendant of the Prophet's son-in-law, Ali, the saint is believed to fulfil the wishes of those who have faith. Hundreds of thousands of pilgrims from all over the world come to Ajmer year after year to invoke his intercession in matters ranging from the success of a business to the birth of a son or the advantageous marriage of a daughter.

The narrow road leading to the shrine is lined with stalls and hawkers, and thronged with jostling people, conservative and modern, rich and poor. There are women shrouded in *burkhas*, in swirling saris or trendy *salvar kameez*; Arabs in flowing jellabas, local Muslims in white *kurta pyjama* or more Western clothes; and the distinctive white-clad *khadims*, the servants of the shrine. There is a strong undercurrent of gaiety and hope.

I am a crowd person and come alive in this mêlée. The crush of bodies, the noise, the palpable excitement stir some primitive impulse deep within me. I think it has something to do with the positive vibrations that emanate from a festive crowd, a sort of chain reaction of ebullience. I walk with a positive bounce in my step past stalls selling brilliant *chadars*, coverlets for the saint's grave, glittering with spangles or edged with gold. Others offer souvenirs, video and audio cassettes of the services held at the shrine, medallions and copies of the Koran. A delicate aroma wafts from stalls heaped with pink roses, and stronger scents rise from perfumeries selling incense and attars. There are stalls loaded with Indian sweets, succulent *gulab jamuns* and the rock-hard *sohan halwa*, a local speciality. There is also a tide of sound, voices raised in animated conversation, raucous hawkers and shopkeepers advertising their wares, blaring film music and religious chants. And above it all rises the call of the *mullah* summoning the faithful to prayer. '*Allah ho Akbar*,' he chants, God is great, '*Allah ho Akbar*.'

The crowd surges forward to the shrine and I am swept along with it. I pause with Hemant at the foot of the steps leading to the imposing entrance and let the flood of people wash past. We are besieged by *khadims* who live off what they earn from the pilgrims. In order to avoid the unpleasant feeling of being taken for a ride, I have asked the tourist office to recommend a *khadim*, and he eventually arrives. He is tall and very refined, and looks at his big gold wristwatch repeatedly.

'I am very busy,' he says, a frown creasing his forehead, 'I have so many VIPs to take around the shrine. We must rush. A judge from the High Court is coming soon, but I will give you all informations.'

He talks rapidly in a well-rehearsed but informative patter

with lengthy explanations about who built what when. I keep telling him that I am not interested in this kind of detail, that I would really like to hear more about Sufism and Khwaja Muin-ud-din Chishti. I have always been attracted to Sufism's doctrine of love and equality, and also to its mysticism, that elusive quality which modern religion has largely lost.

The word 'sufi', which derives from the Persian word for wool, *suf*, refers to the rough woollen shirts worn by Sufi penitents, rather like the hair shirts of Christianity. The sect developed in the eighth century in reaction against the growing worldliness among Muslims and the emphasis on rigid religious practices. Sufis advocate the love of God as the only path and follow a series of practices to transcend the world in order to focus only on this truth. The practices include the renunciation of earthly things, a prolonged period of penance, instruction under a *pir* (or saint) until revelation occurs (described evocatively as 'a lifting of the veil') and the final and deeply emotional phase of ecstatic communion with God. Hypnotic techniques such as chants, songs and dance induce a trance or heightened state of being, when the worshipper becomes *fida*, lost in God.

I ask our *khadim* how the saint was able to convert thousands of people in a very short time. 'The most important characteristic of the Chishti order, the foremost of all Sufi orders, is its emphasis on the equality of all men, on brotherhood, irrespective of caste or creed. Most of the saint's followers, Islam's first converts in India, were poor people, and he was called Khwaja Sahib, protector of the poor.'

Among his more celebrated followers were the Moghul

emperors. 'Akbar,' the *khadim* tells me, 'walked on two occasions from Agra to Ajmer in thanksgiving for boons received. Such was the emperor's reverence for Khwaja Sahib that even his battle cry, *Ya Muin*, recalled his name. He built markers along the road from Agra to guide pilgrims to Ajmer; many can be seen to this day.'

The Meo tribe, who lived in the area around Patan, were among Khwaja Sahib's earliest converts. Majeedan, from our farm, has asked me to offer a *chadar* for the saint on her behalf and given me a hundred and one rupees to pay for it. It is a vast sum of money for her, an act of love and faith. Since I am completely ignorant of the customs and rituals of Islam, our *khadim* helps me purchase a *chadar* for her. I settle for a green and gold brocaded coverlet with touches of bright red that I think Majeedan would like. It is put into a basket which, I am told, I must carry on my head. With it is a basket of rose petals, also to be carried on my head. I pose self-consciously with both baskets precariously balanced and ask Hemant to take a photograph for Majeedan.

It occurs to me that the hundred and one rupees I have paid for the lot would not begin to cover the cost of the rich fabric of the *chadar*. 'That's because they are resold,' explains our *khadim*. 'Thousands of *chadars* are offered every day and it would be impossible to keep them all, so they are left on the tomb for a while and then taken back to the shop.' The explanation makes very good sense but it leaves me feeling strangely let down.

The *khadim* rushes us to the shrine, looking at his wristwatch every few minutes. There are many places where I would like to linger and many people with whom I would like to speak, but he insists that I do all the lingering and talking after he has shown us around, given us the information and conducted the ritual for Majeedan. I ask him repeatedly to find me someone who does have the time, but he ignores me and continues to rattle off information that I am not interested in or am simply too angry to absorb. Bad feelings with which to enter a holy place.

Originally a simple brick tomb, the mausoleum has expanded over the centuries thanks to the lavish gifts of wealthy and powerful devotees; it is now a large complex of mosques, pavilions and gateways. I try to quieten my mind as we approach the shrine and join the throng of pilgrims walking around the tomb, which is enclosed by a silver railing. Hemant, wearing a knotted handkerchief on his head instead of the cap worn by most Muslim men, whispers, 'Between ten and twenty thousand pilgrims are said to visit the tomb every day.'

Our *khadim*, who has hopped into the sacred enclosure, calls me over to the railing. He takes the *chadar* and hands me the flowers. 'Throw them onto the tomb,' he instructs, 'and ask for whatever you want and it will be granted.' I throw the rose petals: one handful for Majeedan, another for her married daughter, Morvi, a third for her lame son, Joru, a fourth for the two little ones, Jorvi and Irfan, and with the last I include wishes for my own family. The *khadim* tosses the *chadar* over my head and chants prayers for the fulfilment of my intentions. 'For Majeedan too,' I remind him, 'for Majeedan too.' But I suspect he ignores me; Khwaja Sahib, though, will have heard.

AJMER

I receive a handful of sugared sweets, blest food that is more usually associated with Hinduism than with Islam, and am further surprised when the *khadim* ties a typically Hindu red and orange thread around my wrist. Obviously another borrowed custom.

We circumambulate the shrine again and are ushered out by a side door. We stop to listen to a local group of singers who sit on mats outside the shrine, singing to the saint. The music is easy to relate to; it has verve and enthusiasm and there is a hypnotic percussive accompaniment. The repetitive phrases of the *qawwalis*, or devotional songs, are easy to follow, and I find myself clapping and swaying. It is easy to understand how this kind of music, which often continues for hours, would open the mind and the soul. One of the singers, more overcome than the others, gets up and begins to dance, stamping and swirling in time to the music. His movements are so abandoned that his *kurta* rips at the shoulder, his white skullcap flies off and his prayer beads fall to the ground. But he notices none of these things. His eyes are glazed; he is lost in God.

There have even been occasions, the *khadim* tells me, when Sufis have died during this state of ecstasy. 'One couplet that inspired such a death was particularly beautiful,' he says, and for a moment a gentleness softens his brusque demeanour. He quotes, ' "For the victims of the sword of Divine Love, there is a new life every moment from the unseen." Beautiful, isn't it?' he smiles, transformed.

Once there were *qawwalis* almost every day, but the Hindi cinema has lured many singers away, and some of the best

85

migrated to Pakistan during Partition. The *khadim*, towards whom I now feel more kindly, is looking worried again. I suggest that since he has shown us around, he can now leave us and get on with his other appointments. He smiles in relief and we say our farewells.

I look around for a place to sit for a while, and my eye is caught by the arched façade and restrained lines of a white marble mosque built by Shah Jehan. Several old men sit under its exquisitely proportioned colonnade in deep meditation; their eyes are closed and they rock gently to some inner rhythm. I sit on the steps near them, lost in my own thoughts.

I grew up as a Roman Catholic, fervently religious as a young girl until I heard the nuns at my convent school refer to non-Christians as heathens and pagans. My father was a Hindu and I found these labels disturbing. Later, when Ajit, who is a Sikh, and I decided to marry, there was a storm of controversy about the rites of the ceremony and the religion of our unborn children. To keep everyone happy we had four weddings: Hindu, Sikh and Catholic as well as a secular one. I saw the Church's insistence that children be brought up as Catholics as perpetuating a sort of club, and I decided to give my children no formal religious upbringing. But my final break with the Church came much later when I was researching Krishna and found that his life story has many parallels with that of Christ. I happened to discuss this aspect with a Roman Catholic priest, a very open-minded man, who agreed there were some similarities, but went on to remind me that Krishna could not be an incarnation of God, as only Jesus

Christ had that privilege. I found the exclusivity, the emphasis on only one way being the right way, unacceptable and offensive.

I am inspired by Sufism's deeply personal love of God – without anger, hate or arrogance – and would like to speak with someone about the religion, but feel awkward about striking up a conversation with people so clearly immersed in prayer. Instead, I walk around the precincts and stop at a shop that sells religious souvenirs to choose a handful of medallions for the people at Patan. The shopkeeper's tranquil demeanour is far removed from the hard sell that characterises the other vendors. He helps me choose, suggesting a medallion that is worn as protection against spirits.

'Isn't this kind of thing at odds with the precepts of Islam?' I ask.

'The externals do not really matter to a Sufi. Anything that quietens the soul and prepares it to flower in the love of God is acceptable. The state of the heart is what is important. Khwaja Sahib did not bring armies with him, he sought only the hearts of the people.'

Ahmed Sahib, for that is his name, speaks slowly and deliberately. 'Love,' he says, 'is the force of life. It can exist only in the complete cessation of desire. When you love someone because that person loves you in return, that is not love. In love you do not ask for anything. You don't even have to seek God, for the happiness that comes from complete love itself is God.'

'That is easy to say,' I interject, 'but difficult to implement, bound as we are by fear and egotism.'

'That is why it is first important to purify the heart, annihilate the self. The intellect is of no consequence to spiritual evolution.'

And when the heart is prepared, when there is no difference between thought and action, then God fills it with love. Ahmed calls it a divine gift. 'It brings joy such as no man knows, and ecstasy. Ecstasy is not just a word,' he says, 'it has meaning, believe me, it has meaning.'

Mouthwatering aromas rise from the small restaurants we pass on the way to our next stop. The rich, fragrant mutton *kormas* simmering in pots and the piles of spongy *shirmal rotis* remind me that it is way past lunch time. I suggest to Hemant that we stop to eat, but he is a strict vegetarian. I walk on with regret.

A flight of steps reaches up to the much-acclaimed Adhai-din-ka Jhompra mosque, described by historians, archaeologists and travellers across the centuries as one of the finest monuments in the subcontinent. There is a robust strength and masculinity about this structure, and it lacks entirely the prettiness that, for me, diminishes later Muslim architecture.

On closer inspection, I discover that the stunning façade of monumental arches integrates the remains of demolished Hindu temples which formerly stood here. It is a monument of transition that superbly combines the divergent structural forms of two cultures: the pillars and beams of traditional Indian temples and the arches of the Islamic world. Mosques were built on temple sites all over India, a process that has since exacerbated tensions between religious fundamentalists on both sides. What many

Hindus forget, however, is that their temples were in turn often built on the sites of demolished Buddhist structures.

Hemant points to some of the looping Arabic calligraphy which scrolls over the façade. 'Someone once translated that for me. It reads, "The Prophet said: For him who erects a place of worship of God with means righteously acquired, Almighty God builds a place in Heaven." '

The key to the quotation, I believe, is the phrase 'righteously acquired'.

Many of Ajmer's monuments date back to the Moghul period, a time of political intrigue and opulence which comes to life for me at Akbar's Palace. Akbar was the first Moghul to conquer Ajmer, making it the headquarters for his campaigns in Rajasthan and Gujarat, and it was here that Emperor Jehangir conferred the titles of Shah Jehan, king of the world, on his son and Nur Jehan, light of the world, on his empress. Dara Shikoh, Shah Jehan's eldest son, was born here and it was also at Ajmer that he was defeated by his brother Aurangzeb in the war of succession.

A window inset above the main arched entrance to the palace is particularly significant. It was here that Sir Thomas Roe, Ambassador of King James of England to the court of the Great Moghul, is said to have first met Emperor Jehangir in 1616, after nearly four years of following the emperor from camp to camp. This meeting led to the signing of an imperial order which gave the British East India Company important privileges in return for the protection of commercial and pilgrim sea traffic from Portuguese fleets. The order laid the foundations of British power and changed the course of Indian history.

I imagine Jehangir setting out from his palace in the state coach presented to him by James I. We travel to Dault Bagh, the pavilions and gardens he built on the banks of the River Luni, in a less regal manner and through traffic that would make the emperor turn in his grave.

White marble pavilions overlook a deep blue lake, set against a backdrop of ancient weathered hills and a foreground of wide expanses of manicured grass intersected by red gravel paths. The form of the traditional Moghul garden, however, is no longer evident.

'This is a park,' says Hemant, clearly puzzled by my insistence on Moghul gardens. 'We have no Moghul gardens in Ajmer.'

I try to explain the Moghul emperors' passion for formal geometric gardens, inspired by the Garden of Paradise described in the Koran. Aghast at the heat and dust of north India, they set the planting of gardens high on their list of priorities. They created gardens of waterways and sweet perfumes, shady walks and massed colour; and Jehangir, a passionate naturalist, was the greatest garden builder of them all.

This would have been a perfect site. Broad sheets of water, such as this lake, cooled the burning wind and soothed the eye, and were central components of their gardens. Water would also have slid along in paved channels that irrigated the garden and divided it into the basic *char bagh*, the four gardens. The pattern would have been reinforced by trees planted along the paths bordering the wide waterways, stately cypresses, representing death and eternity, alternating with fruit trees that symbolised abundance.

I nose around, certain that I will find traces of the original garden. I am not only searching for the soul of this place but also for ideas for Patan. Given the domes and arches of our house and the aridity of our environment, we have decided that a formal garden with waterways and holding pools for irrigation would be most appropriate. There are few surviving Moghul gardens and to find one in Rajasthan would be a wonderful source of inspiration.

Eventually I see traces of it. The high terrace along the lake descends abruptly to a lower garden with a broad waterway lined by trees. At one end of this canal, the city fathers have planted an enormous modern fountain, replacing the jets of water that would have once danced along its surface. I feel as though someone has run a fingernail along a blackboard.

I have been invited to have breakfast with Hemant and his family, and we sit in the rear courtyard of their family home, a cool, leafy place shaded by large, old trees. There are murals on one wall, and a couple of attractive adobe structures. The family runs a paying guest facility for visitors who would like to experience the culture and social customs of an Indian household, and these huts have been designed for guests who prefer a rural ambience. Enterprises such as this have considerable potential as they ensure that the benefits of tourism reach the local people directly.

Hemant's father joins us and his son immediately stands up, and remains standing respectfully behind his chair. 'All those who stayed at my place full-throatedly praised my accommodation, quality of service, food and hospitality,' the older man informs me.

Hemant intervenes from behind his father's chair, a little embarrassed that his father's English is not quite up to the mark. 'We also help our guests experience other aspects of Indian life which, as tourists, they would not normally have access to. We take them to weddings, for example, and on visits to our village home. In a way, my family and I are like ambassadors of India.'

The rental rooms are on the first and second floors, which overlook the city. The family lives on the ground floor: Hemant, his parents, his brother and sister-in-law and their two little girls. The young couple both work in life insurance and his parents take care of the children. A typical 'modern' joint family that hinges on adjustment and compromise, essential when three generations live together.

Hemant puts it well: 'The parents must not be too old-fashioned and the children must not be too new-fashioned. For example, my parents do not expect their daughter-in-law to cover her face, and they also give her full freedom to come and go whenever she wants. She, on her part, gives them every respect and consideration.'

Hemant's father adds, 'Even in big cities, the modern couples are going back to the joint-family system. Because, after all, housing is expensive and many mothers are working.'

Among the system's most significant contributions are the security it provides children and the continued sense of purpose it brings to older people.

'Traditions and values are also passed down,' Hemant observes, 'through myths and legends that grandparents remember and have the time to share.'

After breakfast, Hemant and I drive through a serpentine range of mountains, appropriately called the Snake Mountains, into the Pushkar valley, and I remark on the vastly different examples of geology in the area: mountains, rich green fields and rolling sand dunes. The dunes have largely been planted, except for a few acres where the annual camel fair is held, and my search for the 'real' desert is frustrated. Photographs taken during the Pushkar fair always suggest miles of desert with wind-scooped sand dunes, and I now realise how deceptive photography can be. As a writer, I have long had an antipathy towards the visual media; too often, friends have picked up my books, flipped through them, paused only at the photo sections, and declared, 'Nice pictures'!

In addition to its famous lake and fair, Pushkar is also well known for its roses, which are pink and particularly fragrant. I've told Hemant of my interest in acquiring cuttings for my garden at Patan, and it is to a rose farm that we are now headed.

A small gate leads to a blazing white cottage perched on the highest point of a hill. Acres of roses sway gently in the breeze, the blossoms scenting the cool morning air. The lady of the house is a full-bosomed matron with light eyes and a fleshy, sensuous face. She bustles off to get us buttermilk. It is delicious, lightly salted and flavoured with cumin.

'It's absolutely fresh,' Savitri says, indicating a cow shed a short distance from the house. The floor of the shed is several metres below the ground. 'It's both cooler and warmer that way,' she tells us. 'We have built cattle sheds like this for generations.'

Our hostess settles down on the ground to continue the chore that we had interrupted. A large cloth spread on the floor is covered with dried cauliflower pods, which she pounds gently with a wooden baton to release the seeds. Although the family is wealthy by any standards, and could probably buy and sell all my assets many times over, they do not flaunt their money; nor are they averse to doing menial jobs such as this.

Savitri's son, Satyajit, takes me to the rose fields to show me the plants that will be available after the rains. Roses are a very profitable business, according to Satyajit; over twelve hundred kilos are sold at the *dargah* every day, and many times that amount on special occasions. I notice a low, trough-like structure, rather like a sequence of small open fireplaces. Satyajit tells me it is a series of small furnaces used to distil attar, the essence of roses. The fragrance is said to have been discovered by Empress Nur Jehan, inspired most probably by roses such as these.

I ask if I may buy the tiniest bottle of attar but this year's distilling is yet to begin and there is no stock left over from last year. But Savitri produces a small cough-syrup bottle half full of rose water. My offer to pay for it is met with indignation. I persist but Savitri is adamant, 'You are our guest.'

She tells me to soak some cotton wool in a little rose water and place it over my eyes. 'Any redness will disappear,' she says. 'It's very effective in summer. Remember, the nature of roses is cool.'

It is almost evening by the time we reach Pushkar Lake, one of the most sacred in India and among the important places of pilgrimage that a devout Hindu must visit at least once in his lifetime. We sit outside a café on the edge of the lake, watching the reflections of the white temples quiver in the water. Groups of young tourists and local people drift to the lake's edge in anticipation of the sunset.

The temples were built over the centuries by every Hindu ruling family of consequence, and commemorate various mythological episodes that are said to have occurred here, each endorsing Pushkar's special sanctity. Today, there are over four hundred temples and innumerable *ashrams* where pilgrims stay.

Some locals come by to greet Hemant and linger to talk about the problems associated with the lake. It is silting up: sand blows in every year, and the streams that feed the lake during the monsoons bring in more silt. The government must do something about it.

Hemant comments, 'Surely the people of Pushkar should do something about the silting and not just blame the government. After all, the people here gain greatly from the pilgrims and the tourists.'

'Self-help is the best help,' adds one of the locals in agreement.

'*Kar seva*, voluntary work for God, that is the way it should be done,' says Hemant, brightening with excitement.

Others get the general idea and discussion is enthusiastic. 'If every home in Pushkar could provide at least one person to work voluntarily for a few hours to remove mud from the lake, it could be done without much expense.'

I disengage myself from the animated group and go over to take a look at the collection of postcards which an elderly woman has spread under a large pipal tree. The lady has the build of a retired wrestler, with huge arms and thick wrists, but the rest of her is swathed in a sari and her head is covered.

'I'm a Brahmin,' she tells me. 'This place where you are sitting used to be our ghat. But the lake has receded so no-one bathes here any more. It has affected our earnings badly. Earlier, at least one in ten bathers would make some contribution to us. It's an act of merit, you know, to feed Brahmins.'

Since her children are all grown up and married, and her home is run by her daughters-in-law, she has time on her hands, so she has decided to set up shop to earn some 'pocket money'.

'My husband died years ago. I hated having to ask the boys or their wives whenever I wanted to buy something for myself, so I decided to go out to work.' She points to her postcards spread around the tree. 'My daughters-in-law keep trying to foist their children on me. I like the children but there is a limit, so I tell them that I have no time, I am off to work.'

A customer comes to browse through the postcards. She speaks to him in broken English, and talks him into buying a couple. She turns to me with satisfaction. 'I studied up to the sixth class. When it was time to get married, my in-laws said they wanted a simple, uneducated girl. So my brother told them that I had never been to school and I behaved like a dumb cow for years. Only now do I allow people to see that I do have a brain.' She thumps me on the shoulder to make her point, packing a hefty wallop.

She has raised twelve children. She milked cows, ground the wheat, carried several *matkas* of water from the well twice every day. Today, the girls have piped water and electricity. They have so much spare time on their hands, especially once their children are old enough to go to school, that they get bored and the illnesses start. They need to find some enterprise that they can work at in their homes.

'Why don't you start something?' she says thumping me again. 'Start some tailoring business for export, then all the girls can sew for you.'

I try to explain that I am a writer, not an exporter of garments. 'So what? You can do both. That is the trouble with all you women of today, no enterprise. Start something and you will make money and so will our girls.' This time she grabs my shoulder and shakes me like a dog with a bone.

Rather weakly I promise to think about it and divert her

attention by choosing a couple of postcards, eager to get away. She shakes my hand vigorously, 'Remember, do your project with Brahmin women. There are many schemes for lower-caste women, but everyone forgets our predicament. In the old days, every ritual involved donations to Brahmins and gifts of food and clothing. But things have changed. People no longer follow the rituals strictly and the feeding of Brahmins is now rare. Our women need help. Brahmin women need help.'

She does have a point. Brahmins have been the target of considerable criticism because of the large sums of money they demand to conduct the important rituals that regulate Hindu life from birth to death and which can only be performed by a Brahmin. Now fewer people observe all these rituals and the pickings are leaner. Like other caste groups, Brahmins too are moving towards a new future.

I walk down to the lake and along the shore. A drummer strikes up under a tree, skilfully weaving complex patterns of rhythm. A motorcycle roars up and a young foreigner in a *dhoti* and turban jumps off. He takes over a drum, and a kind of duet competition begins: one player raps out a sequence, and the other attempts a variation. As they play, the sun begins to edge westwards.

People waist deep in water pray facing the setting sun, reciting the sacred Gayatri mantra: '*Asvodityow Brahma*', the sun is Brahma. At the end of each incantation they offer water to the sun, pouring it through cupped hands in an ancient ritual of propitiation to the source of life. The red sun hovers above the spires of the temples, and the volume of the chants increases.

Temple bells peal from across the lake, indicating that evening worship is about to begin. It will soon be time for the *arti* at the Brahma temple. Hemant and I head off in a rush, trotting through narrow streets packed with wares for the tourists: cotton ready-mades, woollen Nehru jackets, waistcoats, mounds of toilet paper and bottles of mineral water.

We are only just in time; the priest is already tending the image of Brahma, lord of creation. He flips a switch and an entire band starts up: cymbals, gongs, drums and a bell. The barrage of percussion, designed to empty the mind, traditionally accompanies such worship; but here the instruments are all completely automated. In a metal cage near us, hammers beat against four brass gongs, six pairs of cymbals chime against each other, wooden mallets pound at two sets of drums and a brass bell rings all by itself.

Hemant whispers, 'It's a time and labour-saving device,' at which point I can no longer contain myself, and laugh till tears run down my cheeks at the wonderment that is India.

Back at Ajmer we return to the puppeteers, who have set up a traditional stage with a dark backdrop and a white awning and skirt. Chairs have been set out and the entire neighbourhood has assembled for the performance. Drums pound out a rollicking beat, and a trumpet blows. Gulab Singh, dressed formally in silk *kurta pyjama* and a magnificent red tie-dyed turban, steps in front of the stage to deliver an impressive prelude to the story of Prithviraj Chauhan.

'The king of Kannauj had a daughter and she was more fair than the fair. Fame of her beauty spread far and wide, and at last it was time for her to marry. Now, in those days parents did not arrange the marriage of their daughters, no they did not. Instead, they assembled suitors and allowed the princess to choose from among them. Following tradition, the king of Kannauj invited all the princes of the realm, from Gwalior, Kota, Bundi, Jodhpur and many other places.' As he mentions the names, regally garbed puppets arrive on stage, parade up and down and then subside against the backdrop.

'The only prince he did not invite was Prithviraj Chauhan, who was his enemy. To further insult Prithviraj, he placed a statue of him in the position of the doorkeeper.' The Prithviraj puppet makes its appearance, soberly dressed as a doorman.

'Royalty needs to be royally entertained,' Gulab Singh continues, 'so Munni Bai performed for the distinguished assemblage.' The courtesan puppet, all in pink with lots of gold sequins, swings onto the stage and commences a bump and grind straight out of a Hindi film that delights the audience.

Heralds shout offstage and drums beat, announcing the arrival of the princess, who is dressed entirely in gold, carrying a garland and attended by two ladies in waiting. Munni Bai is whisked out and the princess walks up and down the row of prospective suitors tossing her head this way and that in theatrical disapproval. She approaches the statue puppet and throws the garland around its neck to indicate her choice.

Having accomplished this dramatic and, for a puppet, difficult feat, the princess leaves the stage. One of the ladies in waiting returns to reinforce her lady's message that she will only marry Prithviraj. Another, more gorgeously attired Prithviraj puppet appears on a horse and dashes up and down the stage. The princess reappears, jumps onto the horse and they gallop offstage to Gulab Singh's accompanying narrative.

Unfortunately, the couple did not live happily ever after: Prithviraj was defeated in battle by the invader Muhammad Ghori and killed. But the puppeteers tell it differently. Prithviraj returns, in chains, with his eyes put out. But help is at hand.

Gulab Singh fills us in. 'Our ancestor, the bard of Prithviraj, sought out his king and reminded him that he would be able to shoot an arrow accurately guided by sound alone.'

The scene changes to Ghori's court. The blinded Prithviraj comes onstage, the bard signals the position of the conqueror by way of a coded message, Prithviraj looses an arrow, and the conqueror drops down dead.

This historically inaccurate version, which reinforces Rajput pride, is one I read in school in a Hindi 'reader', and like every other Indian child I thrilled to Prithviraj's skill and the defeat of the 'bad man', Muhammad Ghori. I did not understand then that this negative image of a Muslim conqueror was a subtle form of indoctrination.

Gulab Singh appears before the curtain again. 'The next part of the programme will be performed by actors,' he announces, and several vignettes that hilariously parody everyday situations are enacted.

One episode satirises greedy and often ignorant medicine

men, and conveys the importance of calling in a qualified doctor. The medicine man having all but killed his young patient comments to the child's mother, 'You are good business for me, how many more children do you have?'

A doctor is called in. He diagnoses pneumonia, and prescribes pills and a mixture. 'Shake it well,' he advises and leaves. The parents hold the child by his arms and legs and shake him vigorously.

Like the others, I laugh till my sides ache. I have never experienced such a powerful tool for social change.

The Moghuls, various Rajput dynasties and the Marathas all gained ascendancy over Ajmer, but it remained one of the few regions in Rajasthan that was never the exclusive territory of any Rajput kingdom. Everything changed in 1857 when an uprising among troops of the East India Company sparked off a nationwide revolt against the British in what Indians prefer to call the first War of Independence and the British refer to as the Great Mutiny. A lack of cohesion among the rebels and the absence of support from many rulers, including the Rajputs, caused the rebellion to eventually peter out, and Queen Victoria was proclaimed Empress of India in 1858.

The British recognised the loyalty of the Rajput princes, and to ensure that it continued they established exclusive colleges to make perfect English gentlemen of their allies' sons. No longer would the princes' education instil Rajput traditions.

One such school was Ajmer's Mayo College, established in 1875 as 'the Eton of India'. I have arranged to speak with the vice-principal, Mr Bhaduri, and before setting out I spent much time searching though my meagre wardrobe for a suitably sober sari. I find that the college is housed in an appropriately magnificent building constructed entirely of unpolished white marble in what is called the Indo-Saracenic style, a hybrid form that attempted to combine Indian and European Gothic architectural traditions in a grand, often wonderfully vulgar progression of domes, minarets and arches.

Mr Bhaduri is a busy man with little time to spare, so we keep the conversation brief. 'The school,' he tells me, 'was opened to the general public only after 1950. Until then only boys from princely families were accepted.'

Since protocol was stringently applied in the princely states, I ask how it influenced day-to-day life at the school. 'It was never a factor in class,' says Mr Bhaduri. 'This kind of institution promotes equality.'

Today, there are almost a thousand boys at Mayo. They govern themselves in the college conclave, presided over by one of the boys. 'The fellow may be a hoodlum,' says Mr Bhaduri, 'but the moment he is in this position, he becomes the personification of responsibility.'

By this time we have reached the big hall, the focal point of Mayo. It is a cavernous room, hung with stern portraits of ruling princes and their coats of arms. A Western music lesson is in rather desultory progress and the boys, in grey trousers and white shirts, jump up beaming at our very welcome intrusion. Mr

Bhaduri is very enthusiastic about the hall, pointing out its two stained-glass skylights, one representing the sun, the other the moon, deities to which most Rajput clans trace their ancestry. The ceiling, painted in what must have been deemed an appropriately royal manner, is attractively executed if a little mannered and stilted, as if the painters, like the staff and students, were not sure to which world they belonged.

I attempt a discussion about the philosophy of education, mentioning that the Indian education system formerly created scholars with a huge range of interests, knowledge and understanding that went far beyond the disciplines they specialised in – whereas the current emphasis on examinations, ambition and competition produces anxious, narrowly focused individuals. But I am not on the same wavelength as Mr Bhaduri. 'When our boys go out into the world,' he says, 'they come out tops.'

Although Mayo now has a sister school, Mayo Girls, in the old days the sisters of many of the boys at Mayo went to Sophia College, which is run by Roman Catholic nuns. I drop in there on an impulse and find a far less regal structure. It is a comfortable building of red brick covered in trails of bougainvillea. Silent nuns with downcast eyes move soundlessly along long corridors around a quadrangle. The mood is monastic and simple.

Sister Agnes sees me in the library, where a class is in progress; the girls are reading extracts from Jane Austen. Sister Agnes tells me that the school is over seventy-five years old and is run by the Mission Sisters of Ajmer.

'Our congregation was founded for Indian nuns only, at a time when few orders accepted them,' she explains in a pronounced South Indian accent that sounds strange in the middle of Rajasthan. She is from Kerala, but a lot of the nuns come from Madhya Pradesh, where the Church has had considerable success among tribal people.

The Right Reverend Henri Caumont and his sister, Mother Matilda, founded the Congregation of the Mission Sisters of Ajmer to carry Christ's mission to the women of Rajasthan. Mother Matilda went on to become the first Principal of Sophia College in 1919. 'The aim was to liberate the women of Rajasthan,' Sister Agnes tells me in all seriousness, swaddled in robes with only her face and hands visible.

Boarding was the secret of Sophia's success, along with the fact that it was run by nuns. Upper-class families felt that the college could be trusted to continue the conservative and secluded upbringing of their daughters, many of whom turned up at the beginning of term in *purdah* cars.

The boarding section has recently been closed, but Sister Agnes doesn't see this as a drawback. 'It is a positive response to the changing environment. Boarding was previously essential to enable us to cater to Rajput girls from far away. Now girls' schools have come up all over the state and it is no longer necessary for them to come to us.'

Nuns pioneered women's education in India and attempted to communicate values they considered important. At the convent I attended, I was allocated a personal motto: Noblesse Oblige. In my day convent education was terribly elitist; all the 'best'

105

people sent their girls to the nuns. There was also the fact that options were limited at the time. Today, convents are less popular because people are not as conservative and there are more schools to choose from. However, more conservative families still send their daughters to 'convent schools', in much the same way as European families send their girls to finishing schools.

Kishangarh is just a short distance from Ajmer on the Jaipur road. A small town, it was founded in 1611 by Kishan Singh, one of the thirty-four legitimate offspring of Maharaja Udai Singh of Jodhpur.

Anyone who is even remotely interested in Indian art has heard of the Kishangarh school of miniature painting, distinctive for its portrayal of women with elongated, heavy-lidded eyes, curved eyebrows, pointed noses, long necks and clouds of dark hair covered by transparent veils. The inspiration for many of these was the courtesan Banni Thanni.

We drive through the town to a lakeside fortress, way off the tourist track, slumbering peacefully in the sun. A white marble palace floats gently on an aquamarine lake. Here Raja Sawan Singh must have gazed with ecstasy on the beautiful Banni Thanni, a slave girl his mother brought back from Delhi. She would have played the *vina* for him and sung sensuous love songs to Lord Krishna in the *bhakti* tradition, which expressed the love of God in human terms.

The intense emotions that bound Banni Thanni and Sawan

Singh were depicted by the court painter Suraj Nihal Chand in miniatures of a rare intensity. He often represented the couple as Krishna and his beloved Radha, for they were both devotees of the 'blue' god, but his most famous work is his portrait of Banni Thanni. Her image reflects his ideal of womanhood, modest and elegant.

Painting traditions continue to endure at Kishangarh, where several signs advertise miniature painting. The Sri Krishna art centre orients traditional painting skills towards commercial production for local and export markets. A young attendant shows me around.

I pause at a large painting of Banni Thanni. 'She is the Indian Mona Lisa,' he tells me in a well-rehearsed patter. 'Observe her enigmatic expression. She is the perfect Indian beauty. A poem describes the ideally beautiful female: her eyes should be shaped like a lotus petal, with an expression as gentle as a fawn; her eyebrows should follow the shape of the bow of Kama, the god of love; her nose should be like the *tilla* flower; her lips as red as a *bimba* fruit; her hair, dark as a cluster of bees; her neck, long like a swan's.' He stops, suddenly embarrassed at having got carried away.

He takes me into room after room, each occupied by painters sitting on the floor, bent over their work. The quality varies from excellent to kitsch, and the painters work on a range of different, sometimes surprising surfaces: paper, cotton, silk and ivory, but also chairs, table tops, boxes and pencil holders.

In one room, the resident 'Krishna specialist' is putting the finishing touches to a painting of the blue god and his consort

Radha entirely in shades of indigo. It is a romantic piece, but what throws me slightly is the fact that the painter is working on four identical pictures simultaneously.

'I find it easier this way,' he says, without taking his eyes from the painting. 'On some days I feel inclined to do just borders, on another it's detailing that catches my fancy, on a third it could be hair or any other aspect of the painting. So beyond the broad basics, I complete the pictures in segments according to my mood of the day.'

The man next to the Krishna specialist is doing a still life, a bowl of fruit in autumnal colours. He too is making multiple versions of the same painting.

'We employ about five hundred skilled painters in and around Kishangarh,' my guide tells me. 'As a result, the interest in painting has surged again. Here you will find people in every village or hamlet painting. Earnings are good too. An average painter makes around fifteen hundred rupees a month, a master craftsman around five thousand. Consider,' he reminds me, 'that the average wage for an agricultural worker is not more than a thousand rupees a month. And agricultural work is seasonal. Adverse environmental conditions, failed rains and ruined crops frequently force people to migrate in search of work. The employment we generate has helped arrest that trend.'

Pichwais are being painted in another room. This is an art form that I particularly like. Literally meaning 'that which hangs behind', *pichwais* are large pictures on cloth which originally hung behind the image in Krishna shrines, designed to evoke the particular theme of the day's worship through incidents associated with the mythology of Krishna. Over the years these have come into popular decorative use and *pichwais* are now often painted on silk, instead of the original rough, homespun cotton. I watch a painter work in broad, sweeping strokes, filling in great swathes of primary colour. Another applies gold leaf, carefully blending it in with the other colours until only a faint glimmer remains.

In the last room, art books from Italy are set out on the floor. A painter is adapting an illustration of a frieze of Grecian columns with a cat crouched on a pillar in the foreground, interpreting it in a more Indian idiom. The effect is strange but not unpleasing.

I rethink the whole question of tradition. The rigidity it implies is negative; to be alive and vital, art must change with the times. It must reflect new economic and social circumstances, and this is just what the painters at the centre are doing. Inspired by both the artists and their enterprise, I ask one of the painters if he has ever painted on walls. It turns out that he is an experienced painter of murals, and we devise a mandala design to cover one of the domes at Patan. Now all I have to do is to sell the idea to Ajit!

CHAPTER 4
CHITTOR

CHITTOR IS the heart and soul of Rajasthan, the wellspring of Rajput chivalry and courage. It was the capital of Mewar for over eight hundred years, before the dynasty moved to Udaipur, and since I am determined to get my historical chronology right, I resist the temptation to linger at Udaipur, where I have arrived by air from Jaipur, and head straight for Chittor. I am accompanied by Devendra Singh, a friend of a friend who comes from Chittor and has kindly offered to show me around the town.

The countryside is lush with crops and I begin to understand why consistent reference is made to the riches of Mewar. I notice fields of white flowers. 'Sesame,' I say to Dev, showing off my agricultural knowledge.

'No,' he says, 'poppies. These are opium fields.'

The car screeches to a halt at my urgent request, and I tumble down a slope to speak with two men at work in one of the fields. If they are puzzled to see a strange woman bearing down on them, they are too polite to let on. Goru, who owns the land, tells me that his family has grown opium for several generations, planted under licence from the state government. In his grandfather's day, a large area of land was under cultivation, but because of the increasing number of addicts, the government is reducing the planting of poppies. Every year the farmers are instructed to plant fewer and fewer, and it is hoped that the gradual phasing out will enable them to adjust to the planting of other crops.

The big, fat pods under the flowers are full of poppy seeds, but it is the skin of the pod that oozes the precious white sap. Goru draws a wire claw-like instrument upwards from the base of the pod, lightly scratching its surface. It is a delicate business that requires experience: just the right amount of pressure should be applied, as the serration should be neither too shallow nor too deep. The white sap oozes out and gradually coats the bulb.

'We usually do this just before dusk,' he tells me. By the morning it has turned black, and is gently scraped off and collected. Fresh serrations are made every evening until the sap ceases to flow. The timing has to be perfectly judged too, so that the markings are made just as the sap rises.

I gesture towards the scarecrows in the fields, white shirts flapping in the breeze. 'The parrots,' says Goru. 'They love poppy seeds and tweak open the pods to get at them. When they peck the pods a tiny amount of sap is released, and over time the parrots become addicted. Then it is close to impossible to keep them away.' He gestures at the overhead electric wires, where several rather drowsy-looking parrots perch, eyeing the field.

The poppy growers often produce more opium than the

amount stipulated by the government and sell the surplus on the black market. Opium fetches between three and five hundred rupees a kilo from the government, and eight to ten thousand on the black market. There are also earnings from selling the husk of the pod, which is brewed into a drink that is used openly all over the country to ward off tiredness. Labourers such as cotton pickers often request that a certain quantity of husks be included as part of their daily wage, and it suits the employer to go along with their demands because the workers' productivity increases.

Goru is not concerned about the morality of growing opium: the thousands of addicts all over Rajasthan are not his problem. I ask whether he takes it, and he answers, 'Have you ever seen a potter drink out of a pot he has made to sell? It is the same with us.'

A similar lack of concern made fortunes for the local merchants and also for the British, who encouraged farmers to grow more and more opium, to the detriment of edible crops. Todd spoke out against the spreading culture of the poppy, and contrasted the mismanagement of the land in his day with earlier laws which stipulated that opium growers plant equal amounts of cane and corn. Opium, he wrote, was responsible for more physical and moral degradation among the local people 'than the combined influence of pestilence and war'.

Quite when or how opium was introduced into India is unknown, and although it was used in ancient times for medicinal purposes, its abuse was widespread by around four hundred and fifty years ago. Todd made an impassioned plea to the East India Company to restrict the growing of opium instead of encouraging it, for 'generations yet unborn would praise us for this work of mercy'.

Dev tells me that in earlier times, few Rajputs drank alcohol regularly – it was opium that gave them their high. Soldiers, who had to travel great distances, kept going on opium and it also vastly enhanced their courage in battle. 'It took the edge off fear,' Dev says. 'Fear causes diarrhoea and opium binds the bowels.'

Over the centuries, opium has acquired wide social acceptance in India. A host will offer his guest opium water from his palm as a welcoming gesture.

'Actually it's rather like having a drink,' Dev explains. 'No-one wants to drink alone, so you nab a friend. And in the way one drink leads to another, so one portion of opium leads to another and another.'

'Surely it is possible to refuse?' I ask.

'It's difficult, especially when it is offered to you by a superior. For example, if the Maharana of Udaipur offered me a whisky it would be rude of me to refuse.'

Today, opium plays a part in all Rajput ceremonies, but is most frequently offered at weddings and after funerals. Even policemen attending a wedding have to put aside their official hats and take a sip.

India is among the few countries in the world where opium is grown legally. It is cultivated to supply pharmaceutical industries both locally and, much more commonly, abroad. The price paid in terms of human life is far too high: in south-western Rajasthan alone, every fifth household has an addict.

We approach Chittor, one of the most evocative relics of Indian history. I squint against the glare and can just make out the fort's hilltop crenellations against the sky. Like most Indians, I grew up on the stories of valour and bravery associated with the fort, where Chittor's kings warded off repeated attacks from neighbouring Hindu rulers and, later, from successive waves of Muslim invaders. The city was sacked three times, but battles lost were transformed into victories of spirit, as each time the women committed *jauhar*, the horrifying rite of mass immola- tion, and the men rode out to die in battle. Chittor's people shed their blood 'in copious streams' over the centuries and their citadel became the symbol of Rajput resistance. The glory of the kingdom of Mewar dates from these times; it was a land literally washed in the blood of her people.

We go straight up to the fort, a complex of arched gates and thirty-three kilometres of walls, wide enough for eight horses to gallop abreast. Within the walls, which crown an entire hilltop, sprawl the remains of one of Rajasthan's most magnificent royal cities, its stately ruins virtually untouched since it was sacked for the last time by Emperor Akbar in 1568. The light is harsh and flat, and I agree with Todd that the monuments wear a 'grey, grief-worn aspect'.

'Chittor is often described as a widow, stripped of her orna- ments, mourning forever,' remarks Dev.

The Tower of Victory, built by Maharana Kumbha to com- memorate his defeat of the Sultan of Malwa, is the focus of tourist activity. A mass of sculpture, awesome in its prolific detail, it depicts every major Hindu deity and myth, as well as symbols from all the other religions of the subcontinent, including the word 'Allah' in Arabic. It is an impressive statement of religious tolerance from turbulent times.

Two girls walk by in swinging calf-length *lehangas*, silver girdles around their hips and heavy silver anklets clanging at their feet. The young man with them wears ankle-high Reeboks and a windcheater. A swirl of skirts, a billowing *odhni* and they are gone, as elusive as the spirit of Chittor is for us today.

At the tank where two *jauhars* are said to have been performed in the face of imminent defeat, I attempt to rationalise the tragic practice. Throughout history, the world over, female captives have been regarded as the rightful spoils of war. To prevent such degradation and suffering, Rajputnis, down to the last female child, entered a mass funeral pyre. Their devastated men, with nothing more to live for, rode out to die in battle. I understand the reasoning, but the reality of the mass immolations is too dreadful to contemplate.

At a temple near the *jauhar* tank, an old Brahmin lady tends to the shrine and packs dried henna into plastic bags, sealing them with an electronic machine. 'See,' she says, unwrapping a carton which reads Mitsumi Polyseal, 'it's made in Japan.'

She is permitted to dispense the holy *prasad* and receive the contributions of the faithful, but she may not conduct the ritual or give the blessing. 'Our religious teachers say that girls should not even read the *Vedas*,' she says with indignation.

Things were different in ancient times: there was no *purdah*. Women attended traditional schools where they studied the sacred texts in Sanskrit and were taught the correct enunciation of the *Vedas* and the mantras. But social mores gradually began to change with the arrival of Alexander's forces in the third century BC, and increasingly so after the first Arab invasions in the eighth century AD. Because it was no longer safe to send girls away to study, *purdah* was introduced and girls were kept at home.

'Naturally, women were unable to learn the mantras properly,' the woman explains, 'and bit by bit our position in society fell.'

Her face lightens with hope. 'But now women are coming into their own again. Look at Indira Gandhi. In our huge country they could not find a man to equal her.'

On the way down from the fort, a small shrine commemorates the martyrdom of Jaimal, a warrior who met his death defending Chittor against Akbar. 'A spot forever sacred in our memory,' says Dev.

Nearby, a crowd of people is gathered around a grandly moustachioed and turbaned man who sits on a satin cushion propped up against rich bolsters, waving a wickedly curved sword over the head of a man at his feet. I look at Dev in surprise.

'I forgot that it's Thursday,' he remarks. 'On Thursdays, this man is possessed by the spirit of Jaimal and heals in his name.'

The supplicant crouches while the healer strikes him on the back with the sword, which must surely be blunt, after which he bends in a deep *namaste* and backs away from the healer.

I sit at the edge of the gathering and watch as a series of other people receive the same treatment. A woman comes to sit beside me. 'Maharaj has great curative powers. I was terminally ill. For years my family took me from doctor to doctor, they spent thousands of rupees, but none of them could find out what was wrong with me. Then I came here for two consecutive Thursdays and I have never been ill since. That was two years ago.'

Today, she has brought her neighbour along. He fell down in a faint one day and was unable to move. Maharaj has given him several treatments and his senses are slowly returning. 'He can crawl now,' she says with pride as her friend approaches Maharaj on his hands and knees. 'It is all a matter of faith,' she says, 'all a matter of faith.'

Dev goes forward to receive the sword treatment in benediction and is then offered opium from Maharaj's cupped hand. He indicates that I too should come to him, and my neighbour shoves me forward. Maharaj brandishes the sword over my bent head, and instead of the opium gives me some milk cake and a handful of fragrant roses.

'I have a surprise for you,' says Dev, looking very pleased with himself as we arrive at an arched gateway. 'This is a traditional school for girls only. I overheard your conversation with the old Brahmin lady at the fort and thought you should see this.'

It is quite dark as we enter to the sound of shrill young voices raised in a ritual chant. A group of girls between the ages of four and fourteen are arranged along the four sides of the courtyard. The only light comes from the sacred fire, which is tended by two young girls aged about seven, their eyes closed as they lead the chant. When they falter, they are gently prompted by a man in white robes who sits by them. The chant is soothing, and all the children rock slowly to the rhythm.

I start as a voice behind me enquires whether I have come to see Guruji. A teenager, very serious and proper, ushers me into a brightly lit room where a saffron-robed man is seated before a low desk on a white mattress on the floor. Guruji is a large man, given to extravagant gestures and lengthy monologues.

'The children's day starts at 3.55 AM, mine at 2 AM. We bathe immediately in cold water, every single morning of the year, and then we all do yoga for one hour, followed by a ritual around the fire like the one you have just seen. Libations of ghee and twenty-five different kinds of herbs are offered to the fire to remove pollution and all kinds of negative vibrations. Eyes, ears and nose begin to water from the medicinal smoke and all pollution is drawn out.

'Breakfast follows: roasted wheat cereal and milk. After this the girls settle down to their work: Sanskrit, mathematics, science and environmental studies. We have classes from grades one to ten, but we can make arrangements for further studies. Three of our girls are doing their Master's and one a PhD.

'There's an hour's break for lunch, a simple meal with nothing that will stimulate the body, just boiled vegetables with some rock salt, a little ghee and a drink of cow's milk. After that it's time for physical exercise. Physical work is good for the soul, so the children do some community work: digging in the garden, working in fields or some similar activity. If there's nothing else for them to do, they carry the benches in and out of the classrooms. By this time it is time for prayers again. The children pray once before eating, and again before sleeping.'

'What about play?' I ask horrified.

'I told you about the exercise period,' he says with some irritation.

What is more, there are no holidays. Once admitted, the children are not permitted to go home until they finally leave school.

'Do you at least allow the parents to visit?' I ask.

'The children don't miss their parents. I am their father and their mother,' Guruji replies.

There are fifty girls at this school and they come from all over the country. One of its ex-students is a lawyer in the Supreme Court, and another is preparing for the entrance examination for the Administrative Service. 'Our girls do very well in whatever field they choose, because here they learn discipline, concentration and dedication. But our main aim is to make our girls like goddesses, ornaments to the homes of their fathers and husbands.'

I declaim angrily about patriarchal systems and the repression of women; Guruji simply replies, 'In which country have women not been oppressed?' He dismisses the subject as not worthy of his attention.

He summons a couple of the younger girls. Their hair is cut very short, 'To avoid lice, you know.' They seem small for their age, delicately moulded with small hands and feet, and slender necks.

My heart aches for them. 'What about love, what about

cuddling, what about parental affection?'

'Ask them,' he says in his loud, hearty voice, 'ask them if they get love.'

The children are standing rigidly to attention. I can't speak, and am close to tears. I finally find my voice. 'Don't you think the children will suffer from culture shock when they leave the school? Children need exposure to cope with life.'

'I told you,' he retorts, 'our girls have concentration and dedication. With that background they can succeed anywhere. We grow up in a world of attachment and desire. These cause all our problems, all our sorrow and suffering. These children have neither.'

I wake to the whistle of a passing train and am reminded of the caravans that once passed through this region. 'Many of them were Banjaras,' Dev tells me over breakfast. 'They were roving traders who also transported the goods of other merchants. Many important trade routes passed through Chittor, and Banjara caravans creaked through this land for centuries.'

My always-simmering interest in nomadic peoples surges to the surface. I am attracted by the concept of journeying constantly, and the freedom it implies; I suppose it has something to do with my own perpetual restlessness. The reality, I know, is less romantic: Rajasthan's many nomadic tribes were compelled to wander because the land simply could not support them. Dev tells me that over two-thirds of the people of Rajasthan remain nomads for this reason.

'What characterises the Banjaras, and almost all nomadic people, is their strong cohesion,' Dev continues. 'I suppose they have only each other to rely upon.'

Listening to Dev, it occurs to me that the Banjaras' personal bonds reinforce their identity, and are their anchor in the absence of physical roots. I had always maintained that much of the enjoyment of travel comes from the absence of responsibility and commitment; perhaps the human condition cannot survive without such ties after all.

Dev interrupts my thoughts: 'The Banjaras are said to be the ancestors of the Europe's Gypsies.'

I snap to attention.

'Some years ago I met a scholar here who was researching the connection. Anthropologists have established that the Gypsies moved out from north-west India in waves and were in Persia by about the eleventh century.' Dev strokes his toothbrush moustache thoughtfully. 'Apparently, their spoken language, Romany, originates in Sanskrit and also has close connections to various Rajasthani dialects. There are many words in common.'

Dev tells me that he knows some Banjaras who have settled close by and we decide to pay them a visit. Dev's idea of 'close by' is at least two hours away, and we drive endlessly, swooping up hills and gliding down into fertile valleys. A river flows beside the road, its sparkling blue waters framed by white sand, dark rocks and distant hills. A man in a white loincloth lays out a long saffron strip of fabric to dry in the sun. Little children and very old men tend herds of goats.

Dev fills me in on the Banjaras as we drive. The traders were a trustworthy people whose word was a sacred bond. 'In the old days there was no insurance,' Dev explains. 'If a Banjara was killed by bandits or wild animals during his journey, as was common at that time, his family would make good the loss.'

The Banjaras often hid their money and valuables along their route, in a small pit in the forest or in a hollow tree trunk; frequently, the location of a Banjara's cache would die with him, and hidden treasure continues to be discovered all over Rajasthan, especially in the area around Chittor.

Some Banjara tribes supplied the commissaries of great armies, carrying grain on their bullock carts. Others traded in salt from the great salt lakes between Udaipur and Jodhpur; the people of Rajasthan once preferred its flavour over sea salt, but now no-one wants it any more, preferring to buy refined salt in packets instead. Unable to move with the times, these less affluent tribes have had difficulty finding alternative employment. Some sell trinkets to the villages; others have wound up as labourers working for a daily wage at construction sites all over India.

The family we are to visit are settled agriculturists and well-to-do. They live a considerable way off the surfaced road, along a rutted cart track. A grove of old trees shades the family hamlet of three or four homes grouped around a clearing in the centre of their fields. The houses are made of mud, and seem to flow from the earth.

As we draw up in front of the hamlet, I notice a lissom girl in her early twenties combing her hair with sensuous enjoyment. This is usually considered a very private part of the toilette in India, and in refined society no woman would be seen with her hair loose. There is a boldness about this girl, an absence of false modesty and a vibrant sexuality. Her young husband watches her mesmerised. Both are completely oblivious to our presence.

An older man comes out of one of the houses; he recognises Dev, and greets him loudly. The girl hastily draws her *odhni* over her head and disappears. Kishan Ram is a hearty man, with a coiled moustache and a shady turban. Like most Indian peasants he wears white. We are lucky to find him, as he has only just returned from Gujarat. He purchased eight cows and bullocks and sold them in a village near Chittor for a hefty profit.

A long journey, I remark. 'That is nothing,' says Kishan Ram, eyeing me with bold curiosity. 'In the old days, armies campaigned the length and breadth of India. And they required supplies: grain, ghee, fodder for their animals and thousands of items for personal use. And the ladies, who often travelled with their husbands, they too required many things. So we were on the move the year round, procuring and delivering supplies.'

They had connections with the Maharajas in those days and supplied them with all their goods. 'There was no railway, you understand,' he explains carefully, as though speaking to a child, 'the railway came later. We used to carry goods from Karachi in the west to Kanyakumari on the very tip of the peninsula.'

'A dangerous life,' I comment.

'We are a brave people,' he shrugs, 'completely unafraid. Even thieves and robbers are afraid of us.'

'For additional protection,' Dev adds wryly, 'many Banjaras persuaded bards to travel with them. Even the most villainous brigand would never harm a *charan*, who was regarded with an almost superstitious awe.'

In a culture where the written word was uncommon, every detail of life was stored in the memory of the bard, whose interpretation of events could either exalt a man to the heights of heaven or stain his reputation forever. The *vish*, the poison of the bard, was feared more than the sharpest sword; his verses could destroy honour, that most precious of all commodities.

Kishan Ram, a little put out by this diminishing of Banjara courage, tells a rather far-fetched story of his people's origins. 'It is said that we were once Rajputs. When they gave their women to the Moghuls in marriage we were ashamed, and so we left and came to live in the jungle. Over the centuries we became traders. *Ban* means forest, *jara* is wanderer.'

But that is all in the past. Kishan Ram's eldest son is a doctor. 'He practises in Gwalior. My younger son is a basketball champion. He is currently doing his MA. What subject he is studying I don't know.' He sighs heavily. 'Both the boys have gone away from our society.'

The younger boy has had offers to act in many films. 'The boy is very good, very handsome too,' says the husband of the girl who was combing her hair. He has a delightful grin and big dimples. 'The film people saw him and they wanted to take him to Bombay.'

'Have you ever seen a film?' I ask.

He looks embarrassed and I'm sorry I asked. 'No,' he says,

and goes off into his fields swinging his transistor radio.

Kishan Ram continues. 'My grandchildren go to a convent school. All nine of them – three boys and six girls. They'll learn to become big people there.' He speaks with mixed feelings, pride but also sorrow.

A group of women standing outside a hut on the other side of the clearing gesticulate to me to join them. 'It would have been inappropriate for us to come to where the men are,' Jamuna says in explanation.

Jamuna is Kishan Ram's wife and the three other women with her, all in their thirties, are her daughters. Tall, handsome women, they are all dressed in *lehangas* and *cholis*, with their *odhnis* perpetually ready to cover their faces. But their *lehangas* are modern versions, in the pale pastels of city fashions. Each woman is laden with clanking silver jewellery. I remark on this to Jamuna, and she summons her eldest daughter and shows me each piece. There is a two-kilo silver necklace around her neck, a girdle that weighs one kilo around her hips, anklets of one and a half kilos on each ankle, plus miscellaneous bangles, bracelets, rings and earrings!

'We each have similar sets in gold,' she tells me. 'Most of it is given to us by our parents. It represents our share of our families' assets.' Contrary to what most men (my husband included!) believe, jewellery is not purely decorative. The weight of an earring, girdle or anklet is believed to exert subtle pressure on nerves which promotes the wellbeing of the body's internal organs.

The young women do not travel with their husbands, as there

are the fields to take care of. 'Surely your sons-in-law don't need to travel any more? The income from agriculture must be good,' I say to Jamuna, gesturing at the healthy crops that surround the settlement.

'Of course agriculture is profitable, the land is rich. But the men have travelled for so many generations. For them, to stay in one place is to get claustrophobia of the soul.'

We drive on deep into the interior, passing through wild but fertile country. I see fields girded by live cactus fences, and where there is water the crops are abundant. Vast areas of common land are liberally sprinkled with stunted trees, their contorted shapes replicating hidden root structures which probe in search of precious water.

Dev has suggested a visit to a hamlet where Kalbelias have settled. These people are hard to define because their occupations have shifted with the centuries. They are itinerant entertainers, snake charmers, traders, mendicants and herbal healers, but also petty thieves. Naturally, they are nomadic.

We drive up to a small group of mud huts in a flurry of dust. The poverty is palpable; there is also a sense of impermanence. An old woman shapes wet mud to form a fireplace, patting the earth until it is firm and smooth. Other women toss grain to remove the chaff, while free-ranging chickens peck hopefully in the dust. Some black and brown goats browse upon the bushes on the outskirts of the settlement, devouring every leaf in sight. A couple of white donkeys stare sleepily into the distance, and men lounge on string beds puffing contentedly on *bidis*. A puppy with a quizzical expression and a hint of greyhound lines comes up to sniff us, and a nice fat baby lies on a mat in the sun. Within seconds of our arrival we are surrounded by delighted children, who study our every movement with frank curiosity.

'These people are expert hunters and trappers,' Dev tells me. 'And their dogs are particularly skilled in hunting.'

I look doubtfully at the bitch standing beside a man with an ancient muzzle-loader. She does have nice lines but stands legs splayed, ears and tail drooping, gazing in a sleepy, lacklustre way at nothing in particular. The man catches my expression and grins, his eyes shifting quickly from the black bitch to me. He bends down to whisper something to her, and she pricks up her ears, muzzle twitching and alert eyes darting in every direction. At another quiet command she streaks out of the settlement, her long legs and streamlined body covering the distance rapidly.

The man laughs at my astonishment. 'We train our dogs to look stupid and lazy. They are among our most valuable assets, we never go anywhere without them. This one came to us as a pup as part of my wife's dowry.'

These Kalbelias used to sell the spindles they made, but few villagers spin their own thread these days and demand has fallen. A familiar theme. Now they travel from village to village selling various items of rural use: bamboo to support thatched roofs, grinding stones, red ochre for the paint which decorates many homes. They travel in large groups carrying their belongings on donkeys or in bullock carts, and while the men sell their wares their women sing and dance.

As with all nomadic tribes who wander among settled people,

the Kalbelias are regarded as pariahs and scapegoats. When they are on the road they often drive off a cow, a goat or a couple of chickens, so whenever there is a crime the police suspect them first. When Dev first came to this village, the Kalbelias thought he was from the police: the men vanished into the hills and the women locked themselves in their houses.

For the moment, all the nomads are at home. 'This is a slack time of the year,' says the man with the dog. 'Several of us have just returned from a long trip. We've made some money, so now it's time to relax and catch up before we go on the road again.'

The women have gathered too and are listening into the conversation. Sita, a small, slender woman with a little girl hanging on to her *lehanga*, joins in. 'Life is hard,' she says, 'but to be overcome by its difficulties is to be buried in misery. So, in the evenings when the moon is shining, we take out our drums and we sing and we dance. We celebrate life.'

'After all,' says the man, 'we are *kal belia*, conquerors of time, of death.'

At the smallest prompting from me, a big drum is produced and tapped experimentally. Sita begins to sing a rather shrill song, instinctively throwing her voice. Other women gather around her, clicking their fingers in time to the music. Unable to resist the rhythm, they begin to dance with graceful, flowing wrist movements and a rhythmic stamping of feet. Dust rises in great clouds, skirts swirl and the dance gathers momentum as more women and several little girls join in.

I have seen Kalbelias dance at stage-managed festivals or in hotels, their movements carefully choreographed; but nothing compares with the joyous spontaneity of this performance. If *I* was searching for the origins of the Gypsies, my money would be on these people rather than the Banjaras.

On the way back to Chittor, we pass an encampment of Gaduliya Lohars. I ask Dev to stop, as it was my encounter with these famous nomadic blacksmiths near Patan that propelled me into taking this journey.

This particular group has settled and built small huts, but positioned in front of each one are the blacksmiths' distinctive carts, surrounded by earthen walls. I cannot conceive of a more powerful statement of their new way of life: they have settled, but their cart remains a proud symbol of identity.

Geeta is sitting in her little mud house making *rotis* over a *chula*. She is about thirty, but weathered and work-weary. She is also very defensive about abandoning the road. 'This is the first time in my life that I have cooked over a *chula*, we always used the same open fire for our smithy and for our cooking. This is also the first time that I have not had to cook out of doors. And my children now go to school, and we have access to doctors.'

She stands up, readjusting her calf-length *kurta*. 'People say that we have compromised the vows of our ancestors. But what are we to do? We need the security of a home too. The availability of work is diminishing, the quality of our work can't match that of factory-produced goods. And as far as I am concerned, I'm tired of a life on the move – of a life where we are regarded as the lowest of the low, where people look down on us and view us with suspicion. Where every petty local crime is attributed to us.'

I ask whether there is anything about the old way of life that she misses.

'Nothing,' she says vehemently. 'Nothing. Can you imagine what life on the move is like for a woman? We have no place to bathe, no place to dress. We must live our lives in the open, like performers.'

Her husband, who has been working a hammer machine a short distance from the house, joins us. 'Our fathers made a grave mistake when they refused Pandit Nehru's offer of free land. After five hundred years of wandering, it was hard for them to conceive of settling, but we are paying for it today.'

Geeta adds, 'Although many won't admit it, all the people of our community want to settle. It's just that they can't afford the land for a house.'

'The real problem,' her husband sighs, 'is availability of work. We have always travelled in a group and when we settle it is also as a group. The bonds are too strong to sever. But if too many of us settle in one place, there won't be enough work for all of us.'

In addition to their vow never to settle and always to wander, other taboos also made life difficult. 'We were forbidden to light even a candle at night,' Geeta says. 'Nor could we own a rope to draw water from a well. Can you imagine how difficult it was to live with these restrictions, when all around us we could see other people benefiting from progress? Are only the Gaduliya Lohars prohibited from participating in change?'

The road to Nathdwara is flanked by a long row of marble-polishing units, and we stop at one to discuss the possibility of installing marble floors in my house at Patan.

The factory owner, Kirit Bhandari, is a pleasant, well-spoken man. He tells me that ninety per cent of India's marble is from Rajasthan, and that the Udaipur region is best known for its lustrous green marble, which is exported all over the world. Udaipur pink is also well known, and is available in tones ranging from bright salmon to translucent pink. A range of whites and greys is available as well. I am like a child in a toy shop.

'Udaipur is fast overtaking Makrana, where the marble for the Taj Mahal was quarried,' Kirit tells me. 'The mines there have been worked for over four hundred years, and are now so deep that excavating is expensive and good material scarce.'

The discovery of new marble-bearing areas and the introduction of machines that can slice marble like cake have brought the stone within the price range of middle-class people. The industry employs over a hundred thousand people in Rajasthan, and is one of the few to have so far resisted the incursions of big corporations, so more of the profits are retained by the local people.

I voice my concern about the environmental consequences of quarrying, and find Kirit's explanation a little too glib. 'Earlier blasting techniques were destructive and wasteful, but modern methods minimise disturbance. Long-range plans envisage the conversion of quarry trenches into natural reservoirs where monsoon water will be collected for storage. This will enrich the micro-environment and will, of course, also be conducive to plantation.'

A geologist has dropped in to see Kirit. He is a man who sees poetry in the movements of the earth. 'The term marble,' he informs me with shining eyes, 'derives from the Greek word *marmaros*, shining stone.'

Millions and millions of years ago, he tells me, the peninsula and Asian land masses moved towards each other in a gradual convergence that convulsed the earth. Their meeting caused conditions of heat and pressure beyond imagination: rocks melted and boiled in the bowels of the earth, and the Aravalli hills that contain the rich deposits of marble were thrust up from the depths. He talks about rocks as though they were people, struggling to survive in a changing environment.

The heat and pressure upset the physical and chemical balance of the rocks and they were metamorphosed into marble. 'It's a beautiful thought that marble was formed from the earth's effort to achieve equilibrium,' he says. 'Don't you find that the stone has a quality of serenity?'

Nathdwara's temple is very famous, very holy and very rich. It is particularly sacred to devotees of Krishna as the home of Sri Nathji, a particularly potent manifestation of the blue god. The temple is said to be the second richest in India, after Tirupati in the south of the country, and attracts pilgrims from every part of the country. Until recently, non-Hindus were not permitted to enter the temple, but now a short ceremony which involves tying a black thread around the neck and placing a leaf of Indian basil in the mouth is considered sufficient to purify the non-believer.

The image of Sri Nathji was brought to Mewar from Vrindavan, the legendary homeland of Krishna, by priests who feared the iconoclastic zeal of the Moghul emperor Aurangzeb. The wheels of the chariot carrying the image are said to have become trapped in mud here, and the priests took this as a sign that the deity wished to take up residence in the isolated village. Renamed Nathdwara, portal of the lord, it grew into a prosperous town thanks to Sri Nathji's pilgrims.

I wander through the outer courts of the temple wondering where to begin. I stick out like a sore thumb because I am a woman alone, and evidently don't know my way about. A man carrying a bundle of brightly coloured pieces of cloth edged with gold bustles by and disappears down a flight of steps. I follow, glad of some direction. A uniformed guard informs me that this is the treasury, a restricted area closed to visitors, and I tell him in the most authoritative tones that I can muster that I have come to see the chief accountant. He obviously takes me for an important donator and ushers me into a room where several men are at work, bent over ledgers on low desks. I settle down in front of the least formidable gentleman, and tell him that I am doing some research into the temple.

His subject is expenditure. 'We spend almost seven hundred million rupees a month,' he says. 'That covers the salaries of around two thousand staff, the cost of the offerings of food to the deity, the upkeep of the temple and so on. In addition, truckloads of offerings arrive every day: ghee, wheat, sugar, rice.'

'What about income?' I ask.

'I am not knowing that,' he says. 'But I have told you the expenditure, you can imagine the income.'

I'm not sure I've got all the zeros right.

A couple have been standing next to me, anxiously waiting to see the accountant. They ask him how much it will cost to pay all the expenses for the noon *darshan*.

'It ranges from two to five thousand,' he informs them.

'Will the five thousand entitle us to sit before the deity?' they ask.

'Yes, yes,' he replies with some impatience. 'The entire ceremony will be performed on your behalf, so naturally you will have precedence.'

The couple step back to confer. The man produces a wad of money and is directed to another accountant. They return in a few minutes, 'We would also like to offer a change of clothes for the deity,' says the man.

'For that you must see the tailor,' the accountant tells them, giving them directions.

Feeling lost, I walk through the outer halls of the temple complex, watching family groups sitting on the floor and chatting animatedly. I miss my own family. Although I have taken this journey partly in order to escape the bonds that tie me to Patan, the emotional ties of family are like great elastic bands that stretch and stretch to allow movement and then suddenly without warning, at times such as this, snap back to Patan, taking me with them.

A temple attendant evidently feels sorry for me in my solitude and offers to show me around. 'Not the shrine, of course,' he says, 'you can only go in there when it opens at noon, but I can show you the rest.' I accept eagerly, grateful for an anchor in this crowd.

'The image of Sri Nathji represents the young Krishna, and it is cared for as a child,' the attendant explains. 'It is ritually bathed, dressed and fed every day. After the food is offered in the shrine it is sold to the faithful, who buy it both for themselves and to feed the poor. We have to provide huge quantities of food; in fact, we have an entire food factory inside. Come, I'll show you.'

Activity behind the scenes is hectic. Men are sweeping and washing floors, and attendants rush here and there with baskets containing fruit and vegetables for the deity. We go up and down flights of stairs into a series of chambers where the food is prepared: in one, vegetables are chopped and shelled; in another, fruit is arranged on platters; betel leaves are wrapped around condiments for *paan* in a third.

'Would you like to make an offering to Sri Nathji?' the man in charge of the *paan* unit enquires hopefully. 'It'll cost you just fifty rupees for a bundle.' I am asked the same question repeatedly as we make our way through the complex.

The flower room is the one I like best, piled high with fragrant heaps of roses, jasmine and marigolds. Groups of men and women sit on the floor stringing the flowers into garlands that will be offered to the deity. There is a quiet, almost meditative quality to this room, in contrast to the bustle and hard sell elsewhere, and for the first time I feel the stirrings of sanctity.

In a room on the top floor of the temple, women cut and grind nuts, raisins and expensive spices behind barred doors. The wonderful fragrance of freshly ground cardamom is pervasive, and I ask my guide if we may sit here for a while and talk. We speak of the many myths that have come together to create the diverse aspects of this complex god: hero, lover, teacher and king. Were these different folk deities amalgamated into a single persona?

To my guide it makes no difference. He is Krishna, the beloved god. 'They say that there are many similarities between Jesus Christ and our Lord. The names, for instance: Krishna and Christ. Then their life stories are similar: both were born in poverty; the parents of both had to flee with the child to escape an evil king, who then massacred all male babies. They say, too, that just as we worship the child Krishna, the Christians worship the child Jesus. Like us they are said to stress complete devotion, complete surrender. And Christ, like Nathji, taught a doctrine of love.' He smiles in satisfaction. 'Our beloved Krishna lived a thousand years before Christ. Perhaps the Christians were influenced by our Lord.'

We move on to visit the temple's many kitchens. One is reserved exclusively for milk-based foods, especially favoured by the god, who grew up in a family of cowherds. Another is for *puris* and other breads. Since Krishna was known for his penchant for sweetmeats, a range of sweets has evolved at Nathdwara and requires a series of specialised kitchens. There are other kitchens for cooking vegetables, for frying and so on.

The variety and amount of food offered to the deity is astonishing: six meals a day, each of three or four dishes, all skilfully prepared for the epicurean god. No wonder the *prasad* at Nathdwara is said to be a gastronomic delight.

It is now noon, and time for the *darshan*. A huge, unruly crowd surges into the shrine as the doors are opened; some pilgrims stop just inside, swaying backwards and forwards with their eyes closed in religious ecstasy, while others push forward to touch the ground before the sacred image.

'Why isn't there a queue?' I shout to my guide above the din.

'The people are moving like a wave in the holy Yamuna River,' he shouts back. 'How does one inhibit the movement of a wave?'

I find another world at Dungarpur, a world that is part of Rajasthan's past and must be part of its future. There are no souvenir shops, no guides, no touts – only a small town with one hotel, an old palace and a lake.

I settle down to relax in the hotel's garden beside Gaibsagar Lake, in the company of some friendly labradors. A graceful, white marble temple sits in the middle of the water, soaking up the sun. Bougainvillea straggles across its walls in a burst of colour, and cormorants and geese perch on its roof, wings spread out to dry. Whistling teal swoop down to join them, brown chests all in a row, and a flock of herons drift across the lake, dazzling white against the blue of the sky and the water. A pair of ducks arrive with a splash while, unperturbed, a white goose bathes, ducking her head and scooping up water in her beak to clean her underwings in a most sensuous manner. Far away on the opposite bank a fisherman casts a net that unfurls in slow motion.

The evening is beginning to draw in, and shades of indigo seep into the sky and shroud the earth. It is feeding time for the geese, and they clumsily descend the temple steps. After swimming to shore with undignified haste, they scramble up the duck walk, cackling raucously like children during school recess. A pied kingfisher in elegant black and white hovers over the lake, wings beating furiously, neck bent at an impossible angle as it studies the water with great intensity. Finally, it folds its wings, drops like a stone into the water and emerges shrieking with a little fish in its beak. It flies to a rock close by, swats the fish against the rock repeatedly and then swallows it, feathers fluffed up with pleasure.

My host, Harshvardhan Singh, was out playing tennis when I arrived; he now joins me, smiling broadly under his moustache. The son of the Maharawal of Dungarpur, Harsh took over the family palace a few years ago, and converted it into this hotel. We move inside, into what Harsh calls the African trophy room. Its walls are crammed with an amazing collage of heads and horns: lions and cheetahs, spiral-horned antelopes and literally everything in between. As much a part of Rajasthan's past as pleasure palaces and war, the relics were collected by Harsh's grandfather, who was passionate about hunting.

Dinner is served in the Indian trophy room, where we talk about Harsh's relative, watched over by sightless glass eyes. 'My grandfather was very much of the old school,' Harsh recalls. 'Protocol was so strict in those days that I had to request permission to see him, and there was never any question of flinging my arms around him or curling up on his knee. That would have been entirely inappropriate.'

The enormous room that Harsh has given me was part of his grandfather's personal suite; the bed occupies only a tiny corner. A balcony leans out over the lake, and inlaid glass in many colours glitters in the windows. I am particularly taken by the dressing room, floored entirely in glass tiles and furnished with clothes pegs along the walls, each sculpted in the shape of an animal.

I sleep in the next morning and am late for my visit to the old palace, the Juna Mahal. The imposing, seven-storey pile has been empty for decades, although Harsh's grandmother continued to live in the *zenana* until her death in the early 1950s. I am shown around by Mahesh Purohit, who has known the palace since he was a child. His father was the chief priest of the Dungarpur Maharawal, and in addition to his priestly duties, he was also responsible for the maintenance and upkeep of the palace, including the restoration of its frescoes, initiated back in 1942.

Dungarpur's golden age was under Maharawal Shiv Singh, who ruled in the early eighteenth century. He was a great administrator, scholar, patron of the arts and, yes, a great lover. As I admire the frescoes which line the rooms of the *zenana*, Maheshji unlocks a cupboard set into the wall.

'This is for sex education,' he says sheepishly, and I bend to take a look by the light of his torch. The 'cupboard' conceals a niche, whose walls are crammed with erotic miniatures. I have never seen such explicit detail; my favourite is of a couple making love while the man takes a pot shot at a black buck.

It's a long drive from Dungarpur to Mohammed Phalasia, where Seva Mandir, a rural improvement organisation, is holding a festival to celebrate International Women's Day. My driver, Udai Singh, has decided he knows a short cut, but what he didn't tell me is that it is a rutted dirt track. We bounce along for hours in clouds of dust, travelling in such slow motion that I begin to feel that I know each fold and crevice of the landscape intimately.

We are obviously lost, but I cannot bring myself to make my irritation apparent. Throughout the drive, Udai has been courteous and helpful, especially protective of a woman travelling alone. And every time he speaks to me, he looks into the distance over my shoulder, for it would be disrespectful to look an elder in the eye.

We stop at a village to ask for directions. A girl who is tending a small shop attached to her family home tells me of an alternative route, giving me precise details. 'It is more suited to a car,' she smiles, and asks whether I am headed for the International Women's Day celebrations. 'The girls at college have been talking about nothing else.'

Uma, I discover, is completing her Master's in Political Science. 'I had a lot of free time,' she says, so softly that I have to strain to hear her, 'so I decided to study further to time-pass.'

She is specially interested in the social responsibility of the rich to the poor. 'Both Plato and Marx tackle this subject. They fascinate me: so dissimilar and yet so alike, even though they are separated by over two thousand years.'

She launches into a comparison of Plato and Marx, detailing philosophical and economic concepts that are far beyond me, so I steer the conversation to education. 'The government is doing a lot for women's education. Also, there are considerable advantages for an educated girl when it comes to marriage. Boys these days prefer literate wives, both because an educated woman is an asset to her family and because she can take a job and contribute to the family finances. More and more women, from rural India as well as the cities, are working, some in government service, others as teachers or lecturers.'

Uma runs an 'Each One Teach One' programme every evening for young girls whose conservative parents do not allow them to attend school. 'The only problem,' she sighs, 'is that not many of the girls are really interested in learning. For most of them it's an opportunity to get away from their homes and have some fun. They either want to gossip or to learn something that will help them earn some money – tie dyeing for instance. They say so what if we can't write our names.'

I reflect on the sobering thought that just one generation ago, girls like Uma would not even have gone to school, and would have been in *purdah* after they were married.

At Mohammed Phalasia, large banners welcome participants to a dusty, open space where a big white marquee flaps in the breeze like an oversized moth. I tumble out of the car to join a large group gathered around a clearing where an archery competition is in progress. All the contestants are women; they are mostly Bhils who, probably for the first time in their lives, are wielding the bamboo bows and arrows their male ancestors have used for generations. The audience, an even mix of both sexes, participates with enthusiasm, applauding wildly when a popular contestant's arrow approaches the bull's-eye and sighing deeply when it misses. This is a big step forward into a male domain, and many contestants are self-conscious and nervous.

A young woman in a blue sari comes forward, the pride and dignity with which she carries herself distinguishing her from the other contestants. She chooses her arrow with care, hefting several in her hand to check their balance, and slowly sights her target. The arrow sings home to the very centre of the bull's-eye.

I remark enthusiastically on her performance to a Bhil tribesman in the audience. 'We never really thought about teaching our women,' he says, scratching his head. 'I suppose it's a good idea, it's certainly a great sport, but what good will it do them?'

I move on to the marquee, and stop to read the slogans written on the banners which decorate it. One translates as 'We are the women of India. We are not flowers but sparks of flame. We are strong, strong and determined'. Another reads, 'Seven generations benefit when one girl goes to school'.

A group of women begin to sing.

My daughter wants, my mother wants,
My mother-in-law wants, my sister-in-law wants,
We all want freedom.
Freedom from oppression, freedom from exploitation,
    freedom from injustice.
It is time for awareness, sisters, time for awareness.

Speeches begin, fiery and impassioned. 'This is a day to make women respect themselves,' says the first speaker. 'We are intelligent, we are hard-working, we are strong – and yet we are to be pitied. Surely something is wrong. We women, who have been sleeping for so many years, have finally awakened to our rights.' Serious faces are lifted to the dais, some shy, some nervous, but all deeply involved. 'But this is not a fight of women against men,' the speaker cautions. 'We want to include our men in the struggle to help their women move forward.'

The speeches continue in full swing, but I sneak off for a quick cup of tea with a group of Seva Mandir volunteers. One of them refers to the exalted position of women in Indian culture. 'A son's supreme duty is to his mother,' he reminds me, 'a brother's to his sister.'

I wonder where it all started to go wrong.

CHAPTER 5
UDAIPUR

I T IS 6.15 on Monday morning, the day sacred to Shiva. The setting sun hovers above the edge of Udaipur's Pichola Lake, and sky and water merge in the flaming reds and pinks of Rajasthan. Maharana Arvind Singh Mewar steps out of his residence, the lakeside Shambhu Niwas palace. He is a teddy-bearish man, with a carefully groomed cleft beard and uncommonly large eyes rimmed by glasses. But what strikes me is the formidable dignity that he wears like an invisible cloak. He is the seventy-sixth descendant of the House of Mewar, scion of one of the world's most ancient dynasties, with a blood line that reaches back fifteen hundred years. He is also the senior-most prince among the thirty-six clans of the Rajputs.

The Maharana is formally dressed in a knee-length black coat, cream silk Jodhpur trousers and a turban edged with gold. Several aides-de-camp and a liveried chauffeur leap to attention and the Maharana sweeps away in a white Mercedes.

I am less ceremoniously bundled into a sporty-looking Land Rover in the company of Rattan Singh, an engaging young man in his late twenties. He wears a perfectly cut dark suit, and tiny diamond and emerald studs in his ears. We are following the Maharana who, like his seventy-five ancestors before him, is making the customary Monday-evening visit to Eklingji, the family Shiva temple twenty-five kilometres away.

Rattan tells me that the people of Udaipur call the Maharana the Son of the Sun, for he can trace direct descent from the god king Rama, hero of the epic *Ramayana*, who was born of the sun. Rattan Singh is also from a princely family, but from a line of younger sons. He does not have the position, the power or the income to match his breeding, but everything in his bearing indicates pride in his identity. He was educated at Mayo, followed by college in Delhi, and now manages one of the Maharana's five hotels.

Rattan was married a few years ago, to a lady with suitable lineage (yes, it was 'arranged'), and he speaks ruefully of the rising cost of living in Udaipur. 'The influx of tourists has pushed prices up,' he says with a worried frown, 'and it's becoming really difficult to meet our household expenses.'

'Does your wife work?' I ask.

'Of course not,' he says with some indignation. 'It would be extremely unchivalrous of me to send her out to earn. It is my duty to support her.'

The Maharana's cavalcade is a familiar sight to the citizens of Udaipur, and the crowded streets clear magically before us. We drive deep into the Aravalli hills that surround Udaipur, their jagged peaks sawing through the evening sky. Called the inner *girwi*, or stockade, they form the natural defences that governed the siting of the new capital of the Mewar region at Udaipur in the sixteenth century, following the final sacking of Chittor. The Aravalli hills bisect Rajasthan and are among the most ancient rocks in the world. Peak rises over tangled peak like a gigantic jigsaw puzzle, in which the pieces never seem to fit, but the evening light is kind and the desolate landscape has a stark, wild beauty.

There is hardly a tree in sight. A few stragglers teeter on top of steep hills like wisps on a very bald head or snuggle into the folds of deep gullies, inaccessible to the most desperate wood gatherer. It is easy to sit back in my comfortable car and condemn the degradation of India's forests, but so many millions of people who can't afford coal or kerosene depend on fuel from the forest for survival. The same forests also sustain millions of cattle, goats and sheep.

A clutch of temples in the distance gleam like a beacon in the gathering dusk: Eklingji at last. The main temple, a soaring mass of honey-coloured granite, is surrounded by the domes and spires of smaller shrines, all glowing with a wonderful grey-brown patina. Their undulating forms recall the Himalayas, which are Shiva's home; there are apparently a hundred and eight shrines, each honouring a different aspect of the god. At Eklingji's main temple, Shiva is regarded as the supreme being: the unborn, unmanifest creator.

The car ahead of us glides to a stop at the old stone temple, and Arvind Singh Mewar steps onto a red carpet laid out in the temple courtyard. Escorted by aides and temple priests, he proceeds directly to the inner sanctum, which is veiled from public view by a red velvet curtain embroidered with gold. There, in front of Lord Shiva, the Maharana folds his hands in personal prayer.

Govind Prasad, one of the temple's priests, whispers to me, 'He is removing the dust of fickle thoughts from his mind, stripping it of all external concerns to enable him to focus on the ritual he will soon conduct.' The priest is short and sturdy, his formidable double chin covered in grey stubble. He wears a purple silk *dhoti* and is bare-chested despite the evening chill. 'My family has tended to generations of Maharanas,' he informs me, his eyes gleaming with pride. 'Their rituals of birth and death, of coronation and marriage, have all been performed by us.'

The curtain before the sanctum is drawn back. The deity is represented by a superbly carved black marble bust with four heads, each of which symbolises an aspect of Shiva, and a large lingam, the phallic symbol of life. The chief priest washes the image with water from the five sacred rivers of India in an ancient ritual of purification which also symbolises the cleansing of the soul. A paste of finely powdered sandalwood, which signifies virtue, is smeared on the image, followed by the offering of a few grains of rice, representing prosperity, and a little pile of betel leaves, which marks the worshipper's readiness to renounce worldly pleasures. Finally, the Maharana garlands the image with flowers representing love, reverence and self-surrender, all the while intoning prayers in praise of Shiva.

Scent sticks are lit and placed on a silver tray with tiny lamps of dough, their wicks dipped in the finest ghee, and the air becomes thick with sweet-smelling smoke. The other worshippers join in the Maharana's chant. Tiny hand-held bells are shaken vigorously, silver trays are pounded with silver spoons and the huge temple bell peals. The cumulative upsurge of sound obliterates thought and empties the mind: there is only the ritual. The noise reaches a crescendo, and is abruptly followed by silence. The Maharana prostrates himself before the deity and touches his head to the foot of the image.

On the way back to Udaipur we pass a small settlement, where a large number of villagers have gathered. Drums beat with an insistent rhythm, and flickering lanterns cast a dramatic pool of light. As usual, I am unable to resist the opportunity to join a crowd.

It is a group wedding, and the grooms are walking with their relatives to the brides' village. Rattan and I join the procession led by a group of drummers: there are flat drums and round drums, single and double-sided drums, all being walloped with more enthusiasm than skill. The procession stops from time to time, and the grooms' young male relatives dance in celebration.

At the brides' village, their male relatives await the procession with welcoming garlands. I have been so carried away with the excitement of the celebration that I only now notice the extreme youth of two of the bridegrooms. I remark on it to my neighbour, an agile septuagenarian who is shaking a leg with the boys, his eyes shining with excitement. 'Four sisters are being married to two sets of brothers,' he informs me. 'The eldest bride is eighteen but the youngest is four years old.'

I express my outrage to Rattan, but his reply is pragmatic. 'You must remember,' he tells me, 'that although the two younger children being married are four and ten years of age, the marriage is in name only. The girls will stay with their parents till they are eighteen. Then, and only then, will they go to the home of the groom. It's like a protracted engagement really. More importantly,' he adds, 'the father of the girls is a potter, a poor man. Marriages are tremendously expensive. The whole village must be fed and so must the groom's relatives. Gifts of clothes have to be made to the prospective in-laws. Instead of incurring the expense four times over, this man has completed all his obligations honourably at one time.'

I think about their realities and mine, and the chasm that separates our worlds. My journey is teaching me many things: most importantly, that I must learn to discard my frame of reference, to listen rather than judge.

My first stop the next morning is the Tribal Research Institute. Udaipur lies at the heart of Rajasthan's great tribal regions, and large populations of Bhils live in the hills which surround the city. Bhagvan Kacchawa, who has carried out an ethnographic survey of Rajasthan's tribes, is a compact man with curled hair and even, white teeth. His associate, Keshav, is very round and bald; he seems to be constructed of circles. 'We are field workers,' Bhagvan tells me, 'not pen pushers.'

This comment piques my interest, since most employees associated with tribal work far prefer comfortable desk jobs. 'One of the problems we face with the Bhils,' says Keshav with concern, 'is that they are bound by the old ways, by superstition and blind faith. For example, they will only go to a doctor if the patient is seriously endangered. All other treatment is done by the *bhopa*, who uses a combination of spells and local herbs.'

I reflect on current theories about the psychology of illness and the increasing interest in herbal cures. Is it really necessary to negate all that is old before discovering that it has some value? On the other hand, it is important not to romanticise tribal life, to remember the realities of hunger and disease.

One such reality, Bhagvan tells me, is the inexorable spread of AIDS among tribal communities. Bhil girls, unfettered by strict social conventions, often take off with truck drivers looking for a little fun and companionship. Tragically, the men are often HIV positive and the Bhil girls and their husbands are infected. It is ironic that a symbol of progress such as the extension of vital roadways brings death and disease.

Tribal development workers such as Bhagvan and Keshav are entrusted with the difficult task of warning tribal communities of the consequences of a little bit of fun. 'The tribal peoples are not very enthusiastic about education,' says Keshav. 'They keep asking us "What use is it?" '

Bhagvan interjects. 'It's not just that they do not want education, it's also a question of priorities and of the difficulties of their existence. They need the children to help with family chores, especially in taking the goats and cattle out to graze.'

'Actually, educated tribals are our biggest problem,' Keshav adds. 'They are neither here nor there. They don't fit into the village or the city.'

'And then there is drink,' says Bhagvan. 'They distil their own liquor from jungle flowers called *mahua*, and even women and children drink it.'

The conversation reveals Bhagvan and Keshav's value systems and, by implication, their conservative backgrounds. 'Another terrible custom is the offering of blood sacrifice to their deities. They offer a chicken or a goat, cut its throat, pour the blood near the deity and then cook it and devour it in a communal feast,' the vegetarian Bhagvan shudders.

I cannot think of a better way of introducing protein into far from adequate diets.

Back at the hotel, I linger over lunch, feeding the chipmunks and sparrows. Jennifer is an old friend of the Maharana's from England, and a frequent visitor to Udaipur. She is a cordon bleu cook and on this trip is teaching the hotel chefs some recipes. Her blonde hair is pulled back into a severe pony tail and she has a brisk, no-nonsense air. She takes off her chef's hat with a flourish. 'There, I'm off duty,' she says with a smile, and settles down to join me for lunch.

She informs me that she has decided to be my guide for the afternoon, and we drive across the city to a lovely walled garden shaded by tall, old trees and crammed with bright, fragrant

151

flowers. The garden is bisected by walkways, beside which water sparkles in channels and splashes noisily into pools. A circular patio screened by a cluster of palms has a fountain in the centre, and as we walk towards it, someone flips a switch and water begins to spout in a fine spray. We sit curtained in a fine mist, accompanied by the sound of falling rain. Saheliyon ki Bari, the garden of the maidens, is one of the most beautiful places I have ever seen.

Jennifer grins wickedly, 'The princes were sent here when they were ten years old to be initiated into the arts of love.'

The 'maidens', of course, were experts in the fourteen arts of love and schooled in the traditions of refinement and sophistication found in the *Kama Sutra* and other such treatises. A young prince would first be taught to make his mind and body desirable. Early lessons focused on conversation, wit and composing poetry and music. Then there was the whole business of the toilette: bathing in perfumed water, anointing the body with fragrant oils, perfuming the mouth with *paan*. Later, he would be taught the art of arousing a woman by the different movements of his fingernails over her soft body; for example, there would be an entire session on how to leave crescent marks on her shoulder as erotic reminders of passion.

Next, there would be lessons on the different types of women, and the prince would be taught how to recognise each by physical and personality traits. This was a lengthy process, as there were twenty-four basic types and a hundred and eight subtypes, and he had to know just how to pleasure each one. Many other things had to be taken into consideration at the onset of a seduction: the phase of the moon, the position of the planets, the time of the year and the manner in which this affected each type of woman. And when he had computed all this, the prince would then know whether to nibble her left shoulder or right, whether to fondle her breasts or tweak a nipple and, most importantly, which position he should adopt to make love.

Jyoti Durga Das grows flowers at her small farm a short distance from Udaipur. She looks as though she has stepped straight out of a Rajput miniature, with fine, regular features and large, kohl-rimmed eyes. We talk about the situation of women in Rajasthan as we drive to her farm, a subject which is increasingly occupying my thoughts.

'Well,' says Jyoti, 'my mother was the first surviving girl child in her family for seven generations.'

I try to sort out in my mind the meaning of what she has just said. 'Female infanticide?' I ask tentatively.

'Yes,' she smiles, 'for seven generations every girl child was killed at birth.'

'How?' I manage to respond.

'Usually by putting a small bag of sand over the infant's mouth and nose minutes after birth. An overdose of opium was another method.'

I swallow hard. It takes me a while to collect myself sufficiently to ask why her mother was allowed to live.

'It was during 1947, during the dreadful upheavals of Partition. My grandfather was in the disturbed border areas and had just escaped a life-threatening situation when a message reached him that a daughter had been born. "Laxmi, the benevolent goddess, has been born to our family!" he exclaimed. "Only divine intervention could have saved my life." ' A message was dispatched that the child must live, and that is why Jyoti is here today.

Jyoti tells me about the social circumstances that led to female infanticide. It all boiled down to that familiar Rajput issue of male prestige, as one of the biggest deterrents to raising a girl was the difficulty of finding her a husband of appropriate lineage. For a Rajput to give his daughter to a man of even marginally lower status than his own was an unthinkable act which would diminish his reputation. A blot on the escutcheon indeed. To maintain their honour – that fragile commodity which so preoccupied Rajputs – families were willing to murder their infant daughters.

I have heard about female infanticide before. Just the previous night, I had read Todd's comments: 'The same motive which studded Europe with convents, in which youth and beauty were immured until liberated by death, first prompted the Rajput to infanticide; and, however revolting the policy, it is perhaps kindness compared to incarceration'. But this is the first time I have actually been confronted by the frightful reality. My mind skitters away from the tragedy, from the thought of thousands of dead baby girls.

Jyoti is speaking, but it takes a while for me to regain my equilibrium. 'My mother was treated as a jewel. She was cherished and loved. After all, she was the first girl in a very long time.'

It occurs to me that Jyoti's mother must be exactly the same age as me. Ajit and I were married when I was twenty-one (without a dowry!), and although our girls followed almost immediately, Jyoti seems much older than our elder daughter. I'm trying to work all this out, when Jyoti tells me she was born when her mother was fourteen. 'Mummy was married at thirteen.'

'And you?' I ask with some trepidation.

'At eighteen,' she laughs merrily.

Jyoti's farm is in a little hollow, surrounded by hills. It's an oasis of rich, dark earth, brilliantly green and radiant with flowers. She lifts a protective sunshade to reveal the incredible sight of enormous double gerberas of every conceivable colour. 'No-one would believe they would survive our harsh summers,' she says with pride, 'but we tend to them with care and love. Plants are my first love, so I thought why not convert my hobby into a career? Udaipur's growing hotel industry will always need cut flowers and at present there are none grown in the area. I also plan to grow indoor plants, for which there's also an increasing market.'

Her project cues me in to the upwardly mobile of Udaipur. Indian families usually look upon flowers as offerings to the gods or as ornaments for the hair, but there is obviously now a niche market for flowers used for decorative purposes around the home.

Jyoti is also experimenting with what she calls exotic vege-

tables: lettuce, baby carrots, cherry tomatoes, baby corn, broc-
coli, Brussels sprouts. We move on to beds of gladioli, huge
double blossoms just past their prime. She has tuberoses too, also
almost finished for the season. 'We've only been working on this
project for a year,' she explains. 'The bulbs are all imported and
terribly expensive. That is why production is limited. Now we
have started multiplying them, so by next year we should have
double the number of flowering plants.' To cover running costs,
meanwhile, there are fields of local marigold, popular among
garland makers.

Jyoti suggests a cup of tea, and as I'm a caffeine addict I accept
with alacrity. As we approach a small cottage, Jyoti folds her
hands in a deep *namaskar* and bows her head before its closed
door. It's a temple to Bhairava, a Bhil deity considered a manifestation of Shiva. The shrine has been here for as long as anyone
can remember, possibly for centuries. 'We tend to the deity,' Jyoti
says, 'and of course the tribes have complete access to the
shrine.'

A row of tribal ancestor stones faces the shrine, all nestled
together under a tree. Each slab depicts a man on a horse and
many are spattered with blood from the offerings Bhagvan had
spoken of. Ancestor stones are erected by bereaved families
when death has been untimely, in the belief that when the gods
take a young life, they allow the spirit to linger and watch over
the tribe.

The ancestors are very important to the Bhils. 'They hold regular
ceremonies here for them. It is a very sacred place,' Jyoti says,
leading me on a few steps further and pointing to an unremarkable-

looking stone. Unremarkable till I notice the sunlight glinting off it. I lean forward for a closer look: the rock is covered with layers of silver foil, applied during each ceremony as an act of devotion. The foil is at least several centimetres thick, consolidated over the centuries, and looks like stratified silver rock.

In a fallow field by the road where Jyoti's car is parked there is a small encampment: three or four tattered tents, little more than bundles of rags tacked together and draped over a few sticks. A small girl about four years old comes running towards us, curious. Around the neck and hem of her very patched dress is a frill of one-rupee coins. I wonder what the coins represent – decoration, saving? 'My sister has them too,' she says, pulling me towards the tents.

Her parents are *saperas*, snake charmers, camping here in the hope of catching a few snakes as they emerge from their winter hibernation. The girl's father has greasy shoulder-length hair. He tells me that the settlement where they live in Udaipur is crowded and hot and swarming with mosquitoes. 'So we thought we'd live out in the fresh air for a while. It's also a good time to collect medicinal herbs.'

Saperas are known in every village for the cures they effect through their hereditary knowledge of medicinal herbs; it is a knowledge they guard jealously. Prime among their curative herbs is one for snake bite, said to save hundreds of lives every year.

Jyoti has another theory about the real reason the *saperas* are here. 'The crops in many places are ready to cut, and I think they are here hoping for an opportunity to steal some grain.' Her comment reminds me of Umardin, Ajit's manager at Patan. A completely illiterate man, but extremely intelligent and very competent, he often speaks of his inherent distrust of the *saperas*. According to him, they let a snake loose in your house and then 'catch' it for a hefty fee. Umardin once called a *sapera*'s bluff by insisting he would kill the snake himself, armed with a stave and a hoe. The *sapera* had capitulated. 'It's my pet snake,' he said, and begged Umardin to spare it.

The snake charmer produces a couple of small, lidded baskets. He takes out his flute, flips a basket open and begins to play, his torso undulating with the music. A cobra uncoils into the classic defence posture, inflating its dramatic hood and swaying 'in time' to the music. I have heard that snakes cannot hear airborne sounds, and that the swaying 'dance' follows the movement of the flute and the charmer's body, while the snake waits for an opportunity to strike.

I mention this to the *sapera*'s wife who is standing next to me. 'Hush,' she whispers, 'talking will distract him and that is dangerous.' As if on cue the cobra strikes, but the charmer anticipates the movement and dances out of reach. The snake continues to undulate, its forked tongue flickering dangerously. Its lidless eyes send shivers down my spine, and I understand why it is said that a snake mesmerises its prey.

The charmer puts his snake away and comes up to join us. He explains his wife's fear. 'We have taken out the snake's fangs, but the poison sacs are still in place. The venom can only be delivered through the hollow grooves in the teeth, and this one's fangs are growing again.'

I mention that people say snakes become weak and sluggish in captivity. 'We take good care of our snakes,' the long-haired man assures me indignantly, 'they are special to the Lord Shiva, after all. We let them go after a year. It's like jail for them in captivity, so it's not fair to make them work for us for more than that time. We feed them well, too,' he continues. 'Even if we can't afford milk for our children, we give it to our snakes mixed with wholemeal flour. Eggs too.' The snake can be fed by soaking cotton in the mixture and squeezing drops into the snake's mouth, but the more popular method is to use the hollow bone of a goat's leg as a feeding tube.

When I remark that snake charming is often condemned as cruel, the *sapera* becomes really angry. 'Now people are trying to say that it is forbidden to catch snakes. They say that snakes are the friend of the farmer, that they help protect the crop by eating the rats. Have you ever seen a farmer's reaction when he sees a snake? He kills it immediately. These policies are instigated by people who live in Delhi, by people who have no understanding of what village life is really like. Snake charming is what we have done for generations. What else can we do? People talk about the suffering of snakes, but has anyone ever thought about the suffering of snake charmers, of the hunger of their children?'

Dinner that evening is with a mixed group of old and new friends. My host was in college with Ajit, and among his many business interests is the export of handmade paper. His petite wife is a

159

beautician and the current president of India's oldest Rotary Club for women. There are thirty-five members, all professional women, seven of whom are doctors. And this is in the heart of Rajasthan!

Another woman at the gathering is a botanist who teaches at the local college, while the woman next to her has made 'special' children her area of study. Her husband works for a government bank responsible for rural finance, and we discuss the long-term possibilities of raising finance from community resources for the women's group I belong to in Patan.

Seated near me are a couple from a small fiefdom near Udaipur. I find them particularly interesting, especially the wife, who is delightfully outspoken. 'I am almost embarrassed,' she says, 'to admit to our princely origins. There is an element of disparagement towards anyone associated with a feudal back-ground. We are discounted as parasites who have exploited the common people.'

Part of the fault, I suggest, lies with the royals themselves because of their flamboyant lifestyles, especially in the earlier part of this century. More recently, many former rulers been unable to cope with the new order, and they live off memories of chivalry and romance. 'That is why so many are also alcohol-ics,' she admits, 'especially the women.'

I knew that many Rajput families were famous for their exotic home-brewed liquors but I had no idea that alcohol was a problem, and certainly not in the *zenana*. But it does make sense. These secluded women were lonely, frustrated and bored out of their minds. They were completely dependent on the whims and favour of their husbands, and often very insecure. 'Even today,' she continues, 'you will find the most conservative Rajput women almost all enjoy a drink in the evening. Whisky, rum and gin, these are the favourites. When we have a formal dinner party, we now have to have a separate bar for the women, who of course sit apart from the men.'

Alcohol is said to have been introduced to the Mewar region by a Maharani who was from a Jaisalmer family. The Maharani had become an alcoholic and many efforts were made to wean her from her habit, but with no success. She became such an embarrassment that it was decided that there was no option but to persuade her to take poison. The Rani was accordingly informed and she asked for a last wish: 'That you, my lord, and your court join me in a last drink.' And, of course, none of them ever looked back.

The insecurity which drove Rajput women to drink was a problem shared by the men. There was so much intrigue and suspicion, so much jockeying for position and power, that no-one trusted anyone. Even the heir-apparent's position and inheritance were dependent on his father's favour, and he often lived in fear for his life. There was also the constant burden of needing to prove their masculinity and superior physical prowess. Hunting, riding and even a game of tennis were all tests of courage and determination, where honour had to be maintained at all costs.

My companion laughs, 'It was hard to be a Rajput woman, certainly, but perhaps not as bad as being a Rajput man.'

Bhagvan Kacchawa meets me early the next morning and we drive out of Udaipur into hilly and increasingly wild Bhil country. Occasionally a few patches of green appear, flashing in the sun, but for the most part agriculture here is rain-fed and meagre. Mud homes cluster together in a series of hamlets that spread across the bare hills.

'Each hamlet represents a Bhil family group,' Bhagvan explains, 'with houses added as sons marry.' I ask if we may stop at one and Bhagvan agrees.

A little child, some three years old, swathed in a shawl the colour of mud, squats in an empty field at the edge of the road playing with the pebbles he has collected in a bright cigarette packet, a prized possession. His mother is preparing the morning meal in the family hut a few metres away. As we peer surreptitiously though the doorway into the darkness within, my attention is drawn to a spotless white calf lit by a shaft of sunlight. A woman inside the hut recognises Bhagvan and greets him warmly, her wizened face wreathed in smiles. Her name is Raju Bai, and she tells me that if I am accompanying Bhagvan, then I am a friend of the family and very welcome to come in.

We bend to enter the low door and a tassel of what looks like dry rope brushes against my forehead. Bhagvan smiles as I start back. This is a special grass that is collected from the forest and hung above each door, in the belief that it protects the animals that pass under it from illness. Realising it must have some medicinal properties, I ask if they can tell me more. But the old knowledge has been lost, surviving only in superstition.

It takes me a moment to adjust to the gloom inside, and to the

162

warm dung smells of the hut that is home to the family as well as its animals. Raju Bai ushers me up a few steps to the next level, which is even darker as there are no windows. All I can see is the glow of a fire and the flash of silver as a woman hunched over it makes *rotis* for her family. She gets up to greet us, wiping her hands on her skirt, and picks up a tiny animal frolicking at her feet that I had taken to be a puppy. It turns out to be a tiny baby goat, born on the same day as the calf, just three days before.

A string bed, the only one in the home, is pulled out for us to sit on and Raju Bai's daughter-in-law hastily puts on some tea. My eyes, now accustomed to the dim light, linger on the spotless floor freshly coated with the mixture of mud and cow dung that is used in most traditional village homes all over India for its antiseptic properties. Brass cooking vessels burnished to a high gloss gleam softly in one corner.

'What happens to these people when they move to towns?' I ask Bhagvan.

'Their standards of hygiene and cleanliness drop,' he answers, without hesitating. 'Here they have identity and pride and status; in the town they are faceless. They lose hope and self-esteem, and eventually nothing matters any more.'

The room is warm and cosy; its thick mud walls and the absence of windows keep it insulated. The thatched roof allows ventilation and some light, but I wonder what happens during the rains.

'Plastic sheeting,' says Bhagvan.

Raju Bai explains further. 'In the past the thatch was changed regularly and it was thick and waterproof. But now the grass required is harder to find, and where is the time? So we keep it in place for as long as we can and manage with plastic in the monsoon. One day,' she says hopefully, 'we'll be able to afford a nice tin roof.'

Her granddaughter joins us and I persuade the three generations to pose for a photograph. Raju Bai wears the traditional full *lehanga*; the silver chains of a head ornament loop over her forehead, and there are heavy anklets and lots of necklaces. Her daughter-in-law is wearing a more skimpy *lehanga* and her jewellery, though similar, is of white metal. The granddaughter wears *salvar kameez* and lots of shiny plastic beads. The difference in their dress is a statement not only of changing times, but also of diminishing resources: there is less money to buy silver or to pay for the fuller *lehangas*.

Bhagvan takes me on to the village temple. It is a small stone structure fronted by a deep verandah and a paved forecourt shaded by an old pipal tree. The tribal priest, a *bhopa* whose name is Gomaji, accompanies us into the shrine. He is tall, with a nut-brown face and burning black eyes. During the working week he is a master mason and is paid a hundred rupees a day; on Saturdays and Sundays he does not go to work, but comes here to serve the gods.

Bhagvan and Gomaji embrace joyfully. I have met many representatives of various tribal welfare organisations, and have often been saddened by the attitudes of superiority they assume over the tribal peoples they work with. Such behaviour reinforces differences, and dilutes the effectiveness of projects; Bhagvan, however, displays a warmth and affection that is evidently fully reciprocated.

It is time for the morning ritual, so Bhagvan and I enter the temple. The shrine is long and narrow, and along one wall are several terracotta images of the gods, all brightly painted and decorated with silver foil. A drummer begins to pound a huge double-sided drum and a worshipper beats a brass *thali*, while another rings a large bell which is suspended from the ceiling.

Gomaji, who is squatting with his back against a wall, begins to stir and moan. His thin legs tremble and within seconds his entire body convulses. He reaches for a bunch of iron chains fitted with lethal hooks and flails himself until the blood begins to seep through his shirt. And all the while the drums sound and the bell rings.

The atmosphere is electric. Bhagvan kneels in front of Gomaji, bending low in obeisance. Someone hands the *bhopa* a bundle of peacock feathers which he flicks over Bhagvan's head and back with increasing vigour.

'He is cleansing him of evil and conferring upon him the benediction of Bhairava,' someone hisses into my ear, making me jump. Raju Bai is standing next to me.

Bhagvan begins to speak with the *bhopa*. 'He is seeking his blessing and asks that his unexpressed wishes come true,' Raju Bai whispers.

'Your desires will be met,' Gomaji says in his strange deep voice. 'But my friend, my old and dear friend, one of the things for which you ask, for which you have asked repeatedly, this I

165

tell you with sorrow I cannot fulfil.'

Bhagvan bows and the peacock feathers are whisked over him again. Gomaji pours a few grains of maize into his cupped hands, along with a few green leaves: the Bhil version of *prasad.*

Raju Bai gives me a gentle shove and I find myself on my knees before Gomaji. I bow my head and feel the whisk flutter over me. I receive the *prasad* and get to my feet feeling strangely beatified. I try to dissect the feeling but my head is full of the pounding rhythm, and I retreat to the back wall.

A young girl swathed in a beige shawl sits cross-legged in front of Gomaji. The ritual is similar but he speaks to her for a long time and gives her a small *matka* of water. 'She is ill,' whispers Raju Bai. 'The water will help her get well.' As the girl gets up, I glimpse a navy skirt and white blouse beneath the shawl – evidently her school uniform. Despite the apparent incongruity, there is really none. The girl attends school, participates in the outside world according to its outside ways; but there is also the way of the tribe, deeply embedded in her soul. The two worlds are completely separate. Both are real.

The drums cease. Slowly the *bhopa* comes out of his trance, and his mutterings fade. He seems to shrink as he squats against the wall, disoriented and clearly exhausted. There is no doubt that he believes he has been possessed by his deity.

Bhagvan unconsciously endorses my thoughts. 'I have complete faith in the *bhopa*,' he says. 'I have experienced miracles here.'

But a shadow falls across his face. 'You must have heard the *bhopa* deny my request. I am issueless: my wife and I have no children. It is with this request that I approached Gomaji, as he is well known for his ability to intercede with the gods for childless people. But it seems that my request is to be denied. I will try again and again.'

The cuisine of the Bedla family of Udaipur is legendary, so I drop in at their home the next morning armed with an introduction. This foray is for Ajit, who is passionate about food and an excellent cook. Kiran Bedla greets me dressed in the typical Rajput *lehanga* and *kurta*, with an intricately dyed orange *odhni*. I address her in Hindi, apologising for the intrusion, and she replies in perfect English. She was schooled – where else? – at Ajmer's Sophia College.

Kiran has regular features and big, dark eyes. She conveys firmness and capability. 'This is a good time to talk,' she says and leads the way to a large, high-ceilinged room, painted an attractive dusky rose.

Kiran's family, who are of course Rajputs, are from Uttar Pradesh, and when she was married she didn't even speak the local Mewari. 'My mother-in-law's personal maids helped me adjust, to learn to understand the ways of my new family,' she smiles in reminiscence. 'They were influential members of the household, who came with her as part of her dowry. I had to touch their feet in respect.'

They also introduced her to the Mewar area's intricacies of dress and cuisine. Various colours and tie-dye patterns are worn

167

on different days. For example, when the sun begins its journey into the northern hemisphere, the women wear yellow fabrics with red and yellow tie-dyed dots. On the full moon, both men and women wear pale pink and white, and a special meal is eaten outside in the moonlight. The meal consists of 'white' foods: mutton is blanched and cooked with milk, almonds and only the seeds of red chillies, while the drink served is a white *arak*.

One of the Bedla family's most famous cooks was a man called Lakhji Barua. He compiled a list of fifty different combinations of spices with detailed specifications on whether they were to be used for roasting, barbecuing, frying or smoking. Many of his recipes have been preserved, carefully handwritten in five hefty tomes that have been handed down for five generations. Kiran browses through some of the volumes, reading out recipes at random. There are nearly five hundred recipes for meat and vegetables, and over three hundred for maize alone. The Bedlas were dedicated meat eaters: even their papadams are made of meat, and they have a meat-based dessert as well.

Lakhji Barua was a master of *pulaos* and almost an entire book is devoted to them alone. The art of Indian cooking rests on these delicate and precise combinations of rice, meat and spices, the mark of a great cook. One recipe calls for glowing coals to be put into the rice and basted with a mixture of ghee and powdered cloves. The coals have to be replaced and the ghee poured a hundred and eight times. I resolve never, never to share this recipe with Ajit.

'The secret ingredient of our cooking,' Kiran says, 'is our own Bedla sauce, a little bit of which is added to many of our recipes.'

It's based on raw mangoes which are soaked in vinegar and a host of other ingredients for around five months, and then ground and strained and mixed with crystallised sugar.

'But the sauce mustn't be made when you have your period,' she warns. 'One of the ladies was menstruating when she was slicing the mangoes, and the sauce putrefied.'

I ask about the family's famous liqueurs. 'We haven't made any for years, not since 1974. But here's a recipe,' Kiran says, still browsing through her books. 'To start with, the wood must be from the wild *bor* tree. There are fifty-four ingredients, ranging from crushed pearls to dried ginger, jaggery, orange peel and saffron. Another has a meat base, and there's even a special liquor for nursing mothers, made from uncured betel nuts. I was given at least one peg every day for several months each time I had one of the children.'

There are heating foods, such as meat, eggs, chillies and fried dishes, and cooling foods, which include curd, raw mangoes, pomegranate juice and garlic. In summer, when the hot winds blow, the recipe books recommend rabbit cooked with onions and curd. There is also an array of cooling mango dishes: meat cooked with raw mangoes, a mango and meat *pulao*, side dishes of mangoes, desserts and drinks. The monsoon is the season of maize, the staple cereal of Mewar, and recipes range from porridge simmered with milk or yogurt to main courses cooked with meat and even desserts. For winter there are heating 'tonic' foods, including pork fat cooked with fried almonds and other nuts, spiced with cloves, cinnamon and cardamom and sweetened with raisins or dried dates. This is given to the children for breakfast!

My taste buds are in overdrive by this time, and it is with regret that I refuse an invitation to stay on for a meal, as I have a previous engagement.

Chandra Bhandari is one of the most attractive people I have ever met. She is small and slight, fragile almost, and yet she conveys an impression of enormous strength, wisdom and compassion. Her greying hair is looped back into a wispy bun, and tiny pearl earrings are her only concessions to ornament.

Chandra runs the women's development wing of the Seva Mandir rural improvement organisation – the group which set up the International Women's Day festival. She has worked in social welfare since the mid-1950s, focusing on the problems faced by destitute tribal women and by urban women living in slums.

During her early years at Seva Mandir, Chandra tried to help women with problems such as wife beating, alcoholism and desertion. 'Soon I realised that was not enough, that it was important to build their capacity to solve their own problems. So we worked towards building confidence, self-esteem and self-respect, to give women the courage to voice their opinions, to take charge of their own lives. We don't want women to be passive beneficiaries; we seek their active participation in Seva Mandir activities.'

Since economic security was essential, Chandra and her staff initiated programmes to help women develop income-generating capabilities: for instance, illiterate women were trained as health workers or taught to run forest nurseries. The next step was to help them gain access to information about government assistance programmes and laws that affect wives and daughters. 'We began to form women's groups,' she tells me, 'which function as information centres as well as support structures.' Now there are over two hundred, each with roughly twenty members.

But Chandra has had to proceed slowly and carefully. Compromise, it seems, is essential to rural development. 'To sustain development, you can't be too radical. You have to go along with the established social norms and chip gently at them, persistently but very gently.

'If a boy is born,' Chandra continues, 'villagers beat a *thali* in joy. The birth of a girl is met with silence. This is just the beginning of an attitude that will permeate the rest of the child's life. It is something that we have tackled seriously, and now in many of the villages where we work, a *thali* is beaten to announce the birth of a girl as well.'

Much later in what has been a long day, I join Arvind Singh Mewar for a drink at his palace, but only after running the gauntlet of several aides-de-camp and signing a red leather visitors' book. The entrance to the palace is dominated by a huge stuffed tiger with a frozen snarl and several life-size paintings of

Mewar ancestors, all with the large hooded eyes and cleft beard of the present incumbent.

I am shown into a large, high-ceilinged room of gracious proportions, crammed with Victorian furniture upholstered in brocades and velvets and smothered in carving. The room is strewn with silver and crystal ornaments, jewelled boxes and many, many photographs of the family with distinguished guests. Miniature paintings and magnificent *pichwais* cover the walls and Belgian chandeliers cascade from the vaulted ceiling. A specially made Persian carpet covers the floor from wall to wall.

The Maharana is a charming host and insists that I try his home-distilled rose liquor, the recipe for which has been a closely guarded family secret for generations. It's rather like vodka, with a hint of sweetness and a faint fragrance. Canapés – stuffed quail eggs, anchovies, caviar and foie gras – are served by a bearer in a white uniform with a scarlet turban and cummerbund, the colours of Mewar. As is so usual in India, Arvind and I discover that we have several mutual friends and we chat comfortably about who is where and doing what.

Inevitably, the conversation drifts to the House of Mewar. Arvind is obsessed with the dignity and honour that characterises his dynasty. 'Among all Rajput kingdoms, Mewar alone never gave its daughters or sisters in marriages of convenience or strategy to the Moghuls,' he tells me with great pride. 'In fact, when Emperor Aurangzeb announced his intention to marry the daughter of a neighbouring chieftain, one of my ancestors rode off, captured the surprised but very willing lady and married her himself.'

Pride in the past has its disadvantages, for Arvind is burdened by the terrible weight of his responsibilities and ancestry. 'In these changed times it is becoming increasingly difficult to fulfil my duties to my people, to maintain the dignity of the House of Mewar which my ancestors have guarded so fiercely. How will history judge me?' he agonises, lighting a cigar to hide his distress. 'No-one wants to preside over the death of a dynasty, be it an industrial house or a royal one reaching back seventy-six generations. It is too awesome a responsibility, this preparation for the future.'

Despite his preoccupation with his heritage, Arvind remarks, 'My feet are in the present and my mind in the future.' Like other erstwhile princes, Arvind is a hotelier. He runs several successful palace hotels in Udaipur, Bikaner and Jaisalmer and owns the fabled Lake Palace. A course in hotel management in Britain helped to prepare him, followed by a stint at a hotel in America. 'I know every section of a hotel,' he says, tapping his cigar into a silver ashtray, 'because I have worked in all of them. I have been a bus boy, washed plates, sliced vegetables and helped in the kitchens.'

Now he keeps a close eye on all his properties, but especially on the two adjoining the palace in which he lives. He bends down to stroke the Great Dane which has ambled in and settled at his feet. 'You could say I live above the shop,' he says with a disarming grin.

But there is a cloud on the horizon. His elder brother, who fell out with their father and insisted on receiving his share of the property in return for legally renouncing any further claim, has rescinded his position. And the brothers, like so many other Rajput royals, are slugging it out in court for the spoils of one of the most opulent eras the world has known. At stake are some of Udaipur's best known landmarks, including five palaces, a hunting lodge, hundreds of acres of farm land, valuable jewels and paintings.

Arvind suggests that I stay on for pot luck, and we sit at one end of a banquet table that seats fifty. 'Pot luck' turns out to be a five-course dinner: vichyssoise, smoked fish, venison kebabs served with vegetables and rice, a chicken dish and, finally, an orange soufflé. All served on gleaming silver.

The conversation turns to the recent past. 'When my grandfather was a young man, he was taken ill with acute appendicitis. The British surgeon from Ajmer was summoned and escorted to Udaipur by a fast fleet of camels. He operated in the hall with all the eyes of the *purdah* ladies looking down on him from a screened balcony above. To calm his nerves during the surgery, he whistled the only tune that came to him: 'Mary Had a Little Lamb', which he repeated over and over again.'

A few days after his royal patient recovered, the surgeon was summoned again and he was asked to whistle the same tune. 'It was recorded onto one of those cylindrical discs. The disc was then wrapped in velvet and kept as part of the treasure of Udaipur, as the magical incantation that had saved the prince's life,' the Maharana tells me, bellowing with laughter.

CHAPTER 6
JODHPUR

THE LONG journey to Jodhpur via Ranakpur takes me through the Kumbhalgarh wildlife sanctuary, a hilly region shrouded in dense deciduous forest that whispers softly in the wind. Many trees are bare and skeletal at this time of the year, but a few evergreens daub the landscape with soothing shades of verdant colour, interspersed with the vivid orange of flame-of-the-forest. One has shed its blossoms, scattering the orange petals on a huge boulder as though in offering to a hidden deity of the forest.

Dusk is approaching, and I instinctively scan the forest for wildlife. A bus roars past and I give up the search, thinking that the disturbance would have driven any lurking creature far away from us. The road spirals uphill in a series of hairpin bends, and as we come around a corner we come across the totally unexpected sight of a panther striding across the middle of the road with great majesty and complete unconcern. Unfazed by our presence, he simply moves off the road and continues to walk with elegant strides along the verge. Udai Singh, who has agreed to drive me on the remainder of my journey, brings the car to a screeching halt, as excited as I am. The panther springs with lazy grace onto a huge boulder by the side of the road, watching us with unblinking eyes, his long tail swishing gently. Too soon, he yawns in bored disdain, bearing huge yellow fangs and a very pink mouth, and bounds off the rock and into the shadowed undergrowth.

I am breathless with excitement. Never in all my years of wandering around forests have I seen a big cat on a main road. Friends had often spoken about such encounters, but I had always dismissed them as fantasy.

The next morning, I am at the Ranakpur Jain temple before sunrise, standing at the base of an enormous flight of steps that reaches up to a soaring mass of white marble blushing gently in the dawn. Inside the temple, hordes of gesticulating gods and goddesses beckon from every niche, pillar and ceiling, each carved with a seductive liquid grace. Female figures dominate, their ample breasts and tiny waists draped in diaphanous garments. Where there is not enough space for figural sculpture, surfaces are smothered with carvings of flowering creepers and fruits.

The impact is cumulative and it becomes all too much to absorb, so I leave the temple and sit outside on the steps watching bus loads of pilgrims come to worship. Most of the men wear *dhotis* and only a shawl over their bare chests, in keeping with the ancient Jain teachings which prohibit the wearing of stitched clothing. The women, however, wear tailored blouses with their saris.

A large, pot-bellied pilgrim joins me in my contemplation. He introduces himself as Mr Mehta, a merchant from Gujarat. Most Jains are in business or trade, he explains, because their religion places so much importance on *ahimsa*, non-injury. In most other occupations there is some violence: for soldiers there is war, and farmers kill insects when they till the land. But there is more to *ahimsa* than just non-injury to living things. 'You see,' he says earnestly, 'violence even in thought is sinful.'

He struggles to explain the Jain tenet of the many-sidedness of reality. 'What I think is right, what you think is right – both are correct. There is a story about five blind men describing an elephant by touching different parts of it. Each described something different, but the perception of each was real. And so, you see, all philosophies are right in their context.'

Another important teaching is *sayyam*, which means no wastage. 'If I can bathe in one bucket of water, why use four? If others are wasteful, we should not follow their example.'

Such teachings were expounded by the twenty-four *tirthankaras*, the Jain prophets who led the quest for release from the cycle of life and the attainment of nirvana. 'To stay pure,' Mr Mehta continues, 'we believe that we should keep busy. Bad thoughts fill the mind when you are inactive. So when you have nothing else to do you should start singing: it drowns out bad thoughts.'

Eight days of every year, he informs me, are devoted entirely to doing the right things. Some Jains remain silent and fast, not even drinking water; those who don't fast eat only non-stimulating foods, 'To keep thoughts from wandering and God in the centre of the mind,' Mr Mehta explains.

Yet moneylending at exorbitant rates of interest is a pursuit synonymous with Jains. 'Surely there is violence in this?' I ask. 'More violence than in eating or drinking the wrong thing.'

'Yes,' he sighs, 'greed is the biggest problem.'

Mid-morning has approached by this time and my stomach rumbles loudly. Mr Mehta grins at me, 'Yes, it is time to be eating.' Lunch has already commenced in the community dining area, where row upon row of wooden tables and benches for several hundred people are set out. The food is Gujarati, with a hint of sweetness in many of the dishes. Many ingredients usually found in Indian cooking are missing: there is no garlic, onion or ginger, nor spices that are considered stimulants, such as cloves. The dominant flavours are anise, cumin, coriander and, especially, asafoetida.

Between slurping mouthfuls, Mr Mehta explains that the Jains' vegetarian diet is based on foods which are freed from the cycle of regrowth, such as rice, wheat and lentils. Rooted vegetables are avoided because they are crawling with the minute bacteria that exist under the earth, and some vegetables are only eaten at certain times of the year; leafy vegetables, for example, are never eaten during the rains, when they often support insects.

In the early evening, Mr Mehta guides me through the temple. We focus on the sculptures, repeated representations of seductive female forms and *tirthankaras* renouncing the material world. 'Man has to experience wealth, luxury and self-indulgence,' Mr

Mehta says, pausing significantly, 'before he can go beyond.'

It finally dawns on me that the opulence of this temple is the expression of all the enticements of the world. 'What is the value in renunciation until there is something to renounce?' Mr Mehta says pragmatically. 'It is from the experience of sin that we evolve.'

Detachment, I begin to understand, is the Jains' answer to life's problems; detachment from the desire which taints all human experience. Theirs is an inner freedom which obviates the need to go to the ends of the world to escape. I am gradually sensing an element of detachment in my own journey: I am able to participate with my senses fully alert, but without the need to possess the moment other than in my memory.

Night has fallen and the temple, which has no electricity, is lit by flickering oil lamps which cast huge shadows. Pilgrims begin to converge, talking loudly and animatedly. The noise is accentuated by priests dressed in red and black who are calling out numbers.

'It's the *boli*, explains Mr Mehta, 'the auction for the right to perform the first acts of worship.'

Bare-chested men with white scarves and *dhotis* are raising the bid, urged on by their anxious wives. The bid goes up to three hundred and fifty-five rupees, and more auctions follow: for offering flowers, for washing the shrine's deity, for covering it with silver foil. A tidy sum is collected.

On the way to Ghanerao the insistent rhythm of drums draws me to a small hamlet, a settlement of the Garasiya tribe, much to the

179

disapproval of Udai Singh. 'They are a feckless people,' he says. 'They can't be relied upon, even as manual labourers, because as soon as they have enough to fill their bellies for the next couple of days, they stop work. Sing and dance, jumping around like monkeys – that is all they really like to do.'

I had seen a group of young Garasiya women near the temple at Ranakpur that morning. They were sitting on a wall, dangling their feet and laughing among themselves. They had radiated a feeling of festivity, of joy in life.

The small settlement is surrounded by fields and lit by a roaring fire. To the beating of drums, men and women dance together before the fire; it is an energetic yet sensual dance, with pronounced pelvic movements by the women and much posturing by the men. Full *lehangas* flare and the firelight gleams on the women's silver jewellery.

I get talking to a worker from Udaipur's Tribal Research Institute, who is a less than sympathetic spectator. 'I am working towards reforming these people,' Madan tells me with a troubled intensity. 'Their marriage customs are very disturbing. Boys and girls meet and mix freely at dances like this and they choose their own spouses. The girls are very forward and they initiate proceedings by offering the boy they like a small gift.'

If the boy is similarly inclined, they arrange to run away. They surface some days later, inform the parents on both sides and the boy pays a bride price to the girl's father – usually around two thousand rupees. If there is enough money to pay for a ceremony, a marriage takes place; if not, the couple live together until the boy can afford the ritual and feast that must follow.

'So what's wrong with that?' I ask. 'It seems a most sensible practice.'

'It is the lowest form of marriage. We call it marriage by capture,' Madan replies, outraged. 'And they don't value the marriage tie. It's usually the woman who leaves; when she tires of a man, even if he is doing his best, she marries another. Only animals change their mates like this!'

Garasiya men, therefore, are very careful to keep their women happy and avoid offending them at all costs. Once, the late Prime Minister Rajiv Gandhi was to visit this region, but he was delayed and night approached. The Garasiya men could not be persuaded to wait, PM or no PM: they were afraid their wives would get angry and leave them. Someone once said that the status of women is one of the best indicators of a progressive society – in which case, the Garasiyas win hands down.

As they dance, the young people sing about the beauties of nature, starry nights, the moon, the hills and the restless rivers. Movements become more languorous, and as we head back to the car I hear a peal of girlish laughter.

It is late evening by the time we approach Ghanerao, and the narrow country road we are taking is crowded with cattle returning home from the day's grazing in the forest. This is cattle-dust time, a time of day that I love.

We follow a herd of cattle up a narrow village street, past the attractive façades of painted *havelis*, to the Ghanerao palace, which glows gently in the golden lamplight. The past lingers here thanks to the absence of renovations or the mandatory coats of paint used to refurbish many old buildings.

An old family retainer guides me into a private courtyard, a little patch of grass overlooked by a pillared chamber that is traditionally furnished with mattresses, cushions and bolsters. Minu, the Rani Sahib, joins me there for a cup of tea. Although in her early sixties, she is still a very beautiful woman; her aquiline nose is studded with a tiny diamond and her complexion is very fair, nurtured by years spent indoors.

'This courtyard,' she tells me, 'was reserved for the men of the family. I saw it for the first time three years ago.' Until then Minu lived on the other side of the palace, behind the fretted screens of the *zenana*. She was in *purdah* for almost forty years; today, she heads the district board which monitors development work in several villages.

One of the first things Minu did when she came out of *purdah* was to start a residential facility for Rajput girls from conservative families, to enable them to attend a girl's school nearby. Because of who she was, the parents were confident that their daughters would be well looked after.

Pressure mounted for her to contest a local government seat which was reserved for a woman. It caused a major domestic crisis: it was unthinkable that a woman of this family could show her face to hundreds of people. 'My husband took eight months to decide, and it caused quite a stir among the local people too. But now everyone has become used to it.'

We talk about her childhood in Jodhpur and school days at Sophia College. 'I went on a hunger strike until my parents agreed to allow me to go to college,' she says, smiling with nostalgia. 'I was already engaged, and since the family I was marrying into was orthodox, my father felt college was not quite appropriate. College made my adolescence wonderful, but it made it more difficult for me to adjust to the restrictions of my marriage. On the other hand, the education I received gave me confidence in this new life, to face large numbers of people, to address public meetings and so forth.'

Minu was married in 1955 at the age of twenty-one and went straight into *purdah*. It was horrible at first, but gradually she began to find ways of continuing her education. She started to improve her Hindi, which was not too good given her English-biased convent education, and she discovered the richness of Hindi literature. 'I also became religious in an odd sort of way. Whenever I was fed up, which was often, I would head for the *zenana* temple. It was one place that it was possible to escape to. I told Krishna everything. I confided every sorrow, every joy.'

In the *zenana*, Minu lived with her husband's female relatives: her mother-in-law, her husband's unmarried sisters and numerous aunts-in-law. Her life was strictly regulated: bathing and dressing, a lengthy process drawn out to fill in the hours, was followed by visits to pay her respects to all the senior ladies, especially her husband's mother.

'My mother-in-law was very dominating, and of course there was no question of answering her back. Any bad behaviour would reflect on my family, and I would take anything, absolutely anything, to avoid letting them down.'

'But how could your father marry you into a home so at

variance with your upbringing?' I burst out, unable to contain myself any longer.

'*Purdah* can be viewed positively as well as negatively,' replies Minu calmly. 'I certainly don't advocate it, but it was part of life in those days. It gave me plenty of time to think, to evaluate, to learn a great deal about life. It taught me how to deal with the most difficult situations life has to offer and I learnt self-discipline.' And control, I think to myself, enormous control.

We continue our conversation over dinner, a simple but well-cooked meal. 'It's ironic,' she says. 'I got married on the 14th of February 1955. And I got elected to public life on the 14th of February 1995. Forty years later.'

Her many duties include monitoring development work in the areas of health and education, as well as identifying various categories of people in need of loans. 'I was advised that I must give the impression that I know everything, but I tell the people I am only an average housewife. By commonsense, intelligence and some very hard work I know I can achieve my objectives. Although I am not trained, I managed a large household, which called for administration, and I am willing to learn.' She smiles her wonderful, luminous smile and the diamond twinkles in her nose.

After dinner Minu shows me around the palace. In one of the sitting rooms I notice a quaint Indian version of a love seat, two stolid sofa chairs, heavy with fringes and green velvet uphol-stery, set front to back. I smile at the thought of a Raja seeking to communicate to a local carpenter the concept of an elegant love seat seen in a richer, more westernised state.

We end up on the roof, the lights of the town twinkling gently below us. We stay there, talking and talking far into the night.

The drive to Jodhpur takes me from the rich lands and forests of Mewar to the barren landscapes of Marwar. The trees are thornier and olive-toned, and ground cover has diminished. Drifts of sand are piled up beside the road, their passage held back by plantations of sturdy, drought-resistant trees, and planted dunes alternate with dry fields which will remain empty until the next monsoon.

A peacock is perched beside the road, its blue neck feathers shimmering in the sun, and a herd of goats nibble at the sparse vegetation. These ravenous foragers are the scourge of the forest department, but they are the poor man's salvation – the source of milk for his family. A field of bright yellow mustard blazes across the land: perhaps someone has struck an offshoot of the Saraswati, the ancient river that once greened this now arid land.

We drive through the wide, dusty streets of a peaceful village, and our pace is slowed by a camel cart laden with sand from the dunes. 'The clean sand is used as a scouring agent. It is cheaper and more efficient than commercial products,' Udai Singh informs me. A white donkey meanders past, its head smothered in pink plastic roses; it is pulling a cart loaded with bottled cooking gas. Sand for scouring and bottled cooking gas: in small-town India, the old and the new appear to coexist comfortably.

Meera and Monty are distinguished long-time residents of Jodhpur. Monty is related to the Maharaja and runs the trust that administers the city's Meherangarh fort; when he has the time he is also a farmer, rather like Ajit. Meera is a distant cousin of mine, and we were all in college together. They live in a gracious old house, furnished in the soothing, clean lines of Art Deco.

I tell Meera and Monty about an excellent book, *The House of Marwar*, which I've recently read. I was impressed by the writer's strong empathy for his subject, tempered by an unbiased rendering of the history, which vividly brought the dynasty to life. 'I was confused, though, by the mix of youthfulness and maturity in the writing,' I say to Meera. 'Do you know how old the author is?' She hides a smile and turns to Monty, who is smirking with satisfaction. The book was written by their twenty-four-year-old son, Dhananjaya, who has just returned from Oxford.

The book fiercely extols Rajput bravery, and I tackle Monty, rather aggressively, on the subject of Rajput honour, as it has been on my mind since my early readings at Patan. Most Rajput kingdoms, including Jodhpur, signed treaties with the Moghuls and became essentially vassal states. Where then, I ask, is their much vaunted honour?

'The joy,' Monty says quietly, 'was in battle. When it was no longer possible to fight for ourselves, we fought for others. That is why most Rajputs were important generals of the Moghuls. We gloried in the fight; the greatest honour was to die in battle. It has been said, and said truly, that a Rajput's dearest possessions are his horse and his sword.'

Whether the Rajputs fought for themselves or for others, it was a question of giving of their best, of fighting to the death if necessary. It was their *dharma*. There are innumerable instances of Rajput bravery under another flag. Under the British, the Jodhpur Lancers fought with distinction in some of World War I's bloodiest confrontations. British regulations at the time did not permit Indian troops to carry firearms, and so the Rajputs went into battle armed only with swords and mounted on horses to fight against machine guns, armoured cars and tanks.

The Jodhpur Lancers really came into their own in Egypt, especially in the capture of Haifa. 'They charged into heavy machine-gun fire with a raw courage that the world has rarely seen,' Monty tells me, visibly moved. It has been described by many as the most remarkable cavalry action in the history of war.

'But to return to the Moghuls,' Monty continues, 'although a lot is made of early Rajput resistance to the Muslim invaders, I don't think it was so much a question of religion as one of protecting one's land and cultural identity.'

This brings us to the subject of marriages between Rajput princesses and Moghul emperors. 'Such alliances were common long before the Moghuls,' Monty insists. 'Just as the men were willing to give their lives, so the Rajput women were willing to enter into these marriages to perpetuate the honour and integrity of their kingdoms.'

Under Akbar, Rajput women were treated with particular deference. One princess even convinced her Muslim husband to shave his beard and stop eating garlic and onions since, as a Moghul chronicler records, 'they were not conducive to kissing'.

Mr Tak joined the air force right after school, and retired with a small pension while he was still young and able. He then went into the taxi and guiding business, and over the years (he is now silver-haired) he found that many visitors, like myself, were tired of palaces and royalty, and so he started taking people out to the villages.

'Many tourists asked me questions about clothing, about turbans and jewellery, so I started specialising in these aspects and now, if I may be so immodest as to say so, there are few people in Rajasthan who know as much as myself. You can say that I am a kind of cultural ambassador,' he beams.

His particular specialisation is turbans. 'We have two main styles in our area,' he says in professorial tones, 'the royal style and the more commonly visible village style. The aristocratic turban is less rounded than the common man's and has a long cascade which shades the back. The other end of the turban is highly starched and stands up in a fan shape over the head.

'In a man's turban rests his honour,' he continues. 'A true Rajput would rather lose his head than his turban, and to snatch your enemy's turban was the ultimate victory. When a king died in a place too distant for his body to be brought home, funeral ceremonies were performed around his turban. In 1678, when Maharaja Jaswant Singh I died in Afghanistan, his turban was brought back to Jodhpur and his queens embraced the flames of *sati* with it.'

Colours are significant too: auspicious red for celebrations, sacred saffron for the final charge on the battlefield, dull green and white for mourning and light pink for the day mourning is lifted.

'Today, the most popular turban in Marwar is the *panchranga*, the five coloured,' Mr Tak informs me. It was designed to mark the current Maharaja's accession in 1952, and sports the five colours of the Jodhpur flag: pink, white, red, saffron and green.

'Among the common people, you can distinguish the region a man comes from by the colour of his turban,' he says. 'A Bhishnoi or a Patel, for example, will always wear white, while the nomadic Rabaris favour red. Muslims, though, usually wear green, to them a sacred colour. Lengths also vary, from eight to eleven metres, and the width is just under a metre. The fabrics range from the finest muslins favoured by the aristocracy to the homespun of poorer people.'

Turban-tying competitions are held at Jodhpur every year. One of the rules of the competition is that turbans must be tied within ninety seconds. 'I always participate and have won the competition so many times that now I am not allowed to enter. Perhaps they will make me a judge this year,' Mr Tak says rather wistfully.

He is also volubly informative about women's clothing, bangles and much else, but it is late and I have another engagement. I tell Mr Tak that I am anxious to visit a Bhishnoi village, and we arrange to meet the next morning.

Like many families in Jodhpur, the Sundar Singhs have converted their home into a hotel. Chandra and Sunder have three children, two girls and a boy. The eldest daughter is married and lives near Pokhran, where she and her husband also run his family home as a hotel. The son is at Cambridge, an advantage that his sisters did not have, but the youngest daughter is able to join us. She is a lovely young woman, confident, poised and with a fresh eagerness.

Priyadarshini helps her mother with the hotel but she also runs an Indian food festival in Switzerland every summer, and has done so for the last five years. When the idea came up through travel agent friends, in true Rajput tradition Sunder asked his mother's permission for his daughter to travel.

'She was horrified that we could even consider sending a young, unmarried girl so far away,' Sunder laughs. He eventually persuaded her to agree by promising to send a suitable chaperone, a female cook who had been with the family since Sunder's mother was a bride. After a couple of months of hectic preparations, Priyadarshini was off.

'It was quite scary at first,' she admits, smiling her open, ingenuous smile. 'Here I was, off on my first trip away from home alone – my first trip out of Rajasthan, in fact – and I was saddled with the additional responsibility of my staff. I had to allay their fears while suppressing mine, help them cope with the experience of flying, which was new to me as well.'

Once in Switzerland, the culture shock was overwhelming. Priyadarshini grew up in the sheltered confines of a conservative and aristocratic family, her mother had kept *purdah* for

190

twelve years, and suddenly she was plunged into an alien world.

The common use of swear words, for instance, was shocking. 'It was unthinkable for anyone to use this kind of language in Jodhpur. Even if men used it in a fit of anger they would never use those words in the presence of ladies. But in Switzerland they swore so freely, and not just the men but the women too, that my ears used to turn red all the time!' she laughs, obviously more worldly now.

'Another thing that surprised me,' she says earnestly, 'was that many of the girls lived on their own, even though their parents had homes in the same city. They used to call their parents sometimes, but the last thing they wanted to do was to visit them. I kept comparing it to Rajasthan, where the family is everything, the anchor of life.'

The free and easy relationship between the sexes was also new to this gently bred Rajput girl, who had never mixed socially, certainly not on her own with men of her age, and whose own marriage will in all likelihood be arranged by her parents. To discover that couples lived together without being married was a huge shock.

'Just recently,' says Priyadarshini, 'I overheard our cook say to one of the new staff, "In Switzerland they are constantly kissing each other, it's their way of greeting. Like we fold our hands and say '*Namaste*.' It's unhygienic, but it's their way. And many times they kissed us also." '

Mr Tak is bang on time, and we head off to visit the Bhishnoi villages. A narrow road leads into flat, open, sandy country. Shrubs edge the track, their ecological significance reinforced in a section of road where they are missing and a large drift of sand lies across the macadam, twitching in the wind.

'This is Bhishnoi country,' Mr Tak tells me, 'you can tell by the *khejri* trees in the fields, which unlike in other areas have not been trimmed for fodder.'

Bhishnois worship the *khejri*, and like so many other Indian beliefs, the tradition is based on sound commonsense. The deep-rooted *khejri*, one of the few species that survive in the desert, provides fodder for cattle and precious shade for houses. Its beans, *sangri*, are a nutritious food, and are dried for eating in summer when little else is available. The tree also binds the soil and absorbs some of the impact of the violent desert storms.

About two hundred and fifty years ago, one of the Maharajas of Jodhpur ordered that a certain number of *khejri* trees be cut for his furnace. The Bhishnois opposed the felling, and many wrapped their arms around the trees and insisted that they would die to protect them. The Maharaja's labourers went ahead and cut down the trees, killing the three hundred and sixty-three men and women who clung to them. An annual ceremony commemorates the sacrifice of these early conservationists.

Environmentalists the world over are now reaching similar conclusions to those arrived at in the fifth century by Jambhaji, the founder of the Bhishnois. The word *bhishnoi* refers to the twenty (*bis*) proscriptions (*noi*) he established, which included sacred prohibitions relating to the cutting of wood, the taking of any life, the gelding of bulls and the drinking of unfiltered water.

Bhishnois fiercely protect their animals and birds and do not allow hunting. A memory surfaces of a trigger-happy teenaged cousin who, while driving through Bhishnoi country, shot a brace of partridge for the pot. In seconds he was surrounded by an angry mob armed with staves and pitchforks.

A chinkara gazelle bounds across the road, followed by another dozen, wagging their tails in excitement. 'The Bhishnois call them *cheenk* – sneeze,' Mr Tak tells me, 'because of their distinctive call.' Plump partridge peck in the sand, and a big blue bull stands among the trees on the side of the road a little further on. He bounds away in disapproval at our intrusion, followed by his harem, who have been waiting in the undergrowth for him to signal that the coast is clear. Small herds of black buck leap through the fields of flowering mustard, their distinctive spiral horns laid flat across their backs and their dark upper bodies gleaming in the sun.

Mr Tak directs the driver onto a smaller track which leads to a cluster of huts surrounded by trees. The huts sit around a central clearing of packed mud, and the façade of each is washed with lime and decorated with paintings of birds and animals. Four women are sitting in the clearing, combing each other's hair. They welcome Tak Sahib as an old and favoured friend, smiling their pleasure. He hugs the youngest woman, pats another on the head and smiles happily. 'I love these people,' he tells me. 'I have been coming here before this one was born.'

The oldest woman – I am tempted to say matriarch but she is probably younger than me – has weathered skin and sun-bleached hair, but her kohl-rimmed eyes are bright and youthful. She tells me she has eight children: four sons and four daughters. The boys are all out at the moment, in the fields with their father, and the girls, all married, are home for a visit.

In accordance with the sacred rules, so Mr Tak tells me, Bhishnoi women wear red *lehangas* with a white rosette and coloured *odhnis*, while the men wear only white. Tak Sahib draws my attention to the big gold nose ring that all the women wear, linked by a thin gold chain to their earring to reduce the weight.

'It is the sign of marriage among Bhishnoi women,' he says proud of his knowledge, 'and is given to them by their husband's family. The round head ornament worn just above the forehead, called the *bor*, is also worn by married women.'

The girls are all very lovely, with clear, fair skins, well-defined features and large, luminous eyes. The prettiest of them, Koeli, is particularly friendly. She tells me that her husband is in the air force – definitely an upwardly mobile occupation. Her *odhni* slips and I notice the hairnet which covers her head; it keeps her hair tidy and also supports the heavy head ornament.

'All four sisters got married fifteen years ago,' Mr Tak tells me. 'The youngest was only two at the time. Group marriages are common among Bhishnois – they save money. Naturally, the girls don't go to their husband's home till they are fifteen or thereabouts.'

Their mother interrupts, 'When the girl is capable of carrying two full *matkas* of water on her head, only then do we send her.' I am charmed by the way she measures physical maturity.

Bhavri tells me that her husband is in the fourteenth class, which means that he is in the second year of college. This family is really going places.

The girls show me around the complex, proud of the cleanliness of their family home. A strange contraption catches my eye in one of the huts. 'It's for mixing opium,' Mr Tak whispers. 'Their father is an addict.'

Bhavri has already settled down to demonstrate. She grinds a pellet of opium which has previously been cooked with some sugar and milk, and then dried. After grinding it, she mixes in some water and then strains the concoction. 'This is for offering to our guests,' she explains.

Their father usually just pops a pellet into his mouth for his high, Mr Tak tells me, popping one into his own. 'I'm used to it, don't worry,' he says. 'When you visit these people as often as I do, it is important to partake of their hospitality. And opium is an important manifestation.'

One of the sons of the family, Jamua, returns. He shares the extreme good looks of his sisters, and a story I have heard about Bhishnois comes to mind. In order to improve their stock, the Bhishnois would choose a boy of about sixteen or seventeen with an outstanding physique, good looks, fair complexion and fine bones. He was called the *nassal sudhar*, the one who would improve the breed. All his sexual needs were taken care of by the village women, and when he left his shoes outside a hut, the woman's husband would graciously stay away. When a new bride came to the village, the *nassal sudhar* probably had first right.

The stud was killed at around the age of twenty-four, possibly with an overdose of opium, in order to avoid any subsequent paternity problems. The custom has, of course, long ceased, but its effects are visible in the good looks of most Bhishnois, among whom there is still a relaxed attitude towards sexual morality. Even today, it is common for a man to come home and find a pair of shoes outside his front door, a signal for him to temporarily retire to another house.

If this handsome family is anything to go by, the Bhishnois' racial engineering has been tremendously successful. We gather over the inevitable cup of tea, and I ask if their reverence for the *khejri* tree extends to replanting.

'During the *mela* that honours the martyrdom of our ancestors,' Koeli explains, 'each Bhishnoi must plant five *khejri* trees. The government supplies them to us free of cost. We plant some at the temple and the rest at home.'

Naturally, the *khejri* is never used for firewood. 'Earlier, there were fewer of us, so dried cow-dung cakes were sufficient for our fuel needs, supplemented by the odd dried tree,' Jamua explains. 'But now populations have grown, and we are forced to burn wood as well. But we only use useless species, the ones that don't allow grass to grow.'

'We also do not cut the *kair* bush,' Koeli adds, 'because from this we get the *kair* berry which we dry and cook with yoghurt. Nor do we cut the *rohira*, as it resists termites and can survive well in the desert which is the kingdom of the termites.'

I ask if there are any particular beliefs that impel them to protect the deer that I have noticed in such large numbers. 'According to our teachings,' Jamua explains, 'if you do good

196

deeds, you will be reborn a deer.'

'That is why we treat the animals as our guests,' his mother adds. 'They eat almost half our crops, but what does that matter? We have the other half.'

'There is a song about it,' Koeli prompts her brother. Jamua obliges and recites some of it.

> *Oh God, after my death don't make me an ox or a horse, they*
> *have to work too hard.*
> *Don't make me a frog either, or I'll have to spend my life croaking*
> *in a well.*
> *Don't make me a dog, please, otherwise I'll be forced to roam*
> *the streets and bark.*
> *Not a pig either, Lord, for pigs live in dirt.*
> *Make me a deer, oh Lord, a free spirit of nature, but please, oh*
> *please, only near a Bhishnoi village.*

Back in the bustling city of Jodhpur, I plunge into the roaring, anarchic vitality of its main bazaar and, as usual, come alive in the intensity of the crowd. Barrows line the approach to the market, their wares reflecting the modest needs of ordinary people, with goods for a few rupees at most. One is stocked with cheap accessories for the hair: clips in psychedelic colours and plastic Alice bands with shiny flowers. The jackdaw predilection for the bright and shiny is so prevalent here that even the ordinary 'scrunchy' is decorated with gold baubles. Another barrow has

Indian-style Barbie dolls with long, black hair and big, black eyes. Others display imitation Ray Bans, scissors and screwdrivers. There are fake Reebok and Nike trainers, bangles, ribbons and handkerchiefs. Larger shops indicate more up-market needs. One sells big, shiny wall clocks with lots of gilt and a prominent range in fluorescent colours. A 'fancy' store sells brassieres and panties. One shop specialises in plastic buckets, mugs and basins; another has stainless-steel and aluminium cooking vessels. At a television showroom several sets have been switched on, and like other passers-by, I too stop to gawk at the multiple images.

Deeper into the bazaar the streets are narrower and even more crowded, and there is the sickly sweet smell of cow dung. A white mare trots by, grandly caparisoned in red and gold for a wedding, and a cow meanders past, chewing her cud with grinding monotony. I follow a herd of small black goats that clatter over the flagstones, returning home after a day's foraging. Vegetable vendors line these streets, catering to housewives who will select their fresh vegetables only for the day's needs. The vegetables are arranged with a fine sense of colour and design, and I savour the sharp, sweet smell of fresh green chillies. A man buys a handful of glistening white horseradish, fresh from the fields. He plucks off the leaves and throws them at my feet. I step back in outraged astonishment, only to be nosed aside by a big brown bull for which the leaves were meant.

The shops behind the stalls double as manufacturing centres. A printer is at work, rhythmically pressing carved handblocks dipped in dye onto a yellow bedspread. He works with accuracy and care, placing each block exactly where the previous impression finished. I watch mesmerised as the pattern unfolds. Around a corner, brass and copper cooking vessels are being silver-plated, and I turn another corner to enter the street of leather workers. This is how it was in the old days: each street was dedicated to a particular craft, with shops-cum-workrooms at street level and homes above.

Jodhpur is famous for its supple leather and fine workmanship, so I stop to buy myself a pair of *jootis*, Rajasthan's traditional pointy-toed shoes. Shabbir Hasan, an award-winning craftsman, is surrounded by row upon row of everyday *jootis*. I wait while he finishes haggling with a customer over the price of a sturdy black pair designed to be worn outdoors. He turns to me with resignation, ready to supply another of his everyday range, but I ask to see his award-winning *jootis*. His eyes brighten, his shoulders square and he crackles with energy, calling out instructions to his son to bring out several pairs.

Shabbir's family, Muslims from Jodhpur, migrated to Madhya Pradesh during a famine, but his father returned about fifty years ago, around the time of Partition, when most Muslims were leaving for Pakistan.

'Our Maharaja announced that Muslims and Hindus were like his two eyes, and harm to any Muslim would injure him personally. He made regular visits to the city to make sure we were well, and although riots rocked the two countries, Jodhpur was quiet. My father's decision to stay was correct, because so many families have trickled back.'

The award-winning *jootis* arrive, narrow and hand embroidered, flamboyant in their beauty. 'Earlier we used to make only these, just a few pairs a year, delicate and as light as the air. But they are expensive and even our aristocratic clients can no longer afford them. The concern now is value for money, not workmanship or beauty.'

More *jootis* arrive, each in its own glass case, and each a piece of art. 'A craftsman,' says Shabbir with great dignity, 'is nothing without the practice of his craft. So I make for pleasure what we earlier made for necessity.'

He is delighted at my delight and places a pair of beige *jootis* with fine gold embroidery on the palm of my hand. 'See how light they are,' he says, and switches on a fan. The shoes fly off my hand. 'They weigh just twelve grams each,' he laughs, exhilarated, 'lighter than a handkerchief.'

Another pair have wonderful upturned toes and the backs are pressed down. 'Moghul Emperor Bahadur Shah Zaffar preferred this style,' he says. 'They're designed to support the feet while walking, yet they're easy to slip off when ascending the throne.' The embroidery on the shoes glows in a hundred carefully blended colours and the tiny stitches are all but impossible to see. 'I make the *jootis*,' he says, 'and my wife embroiders them. This pair took her over six months to work.'

There are slender pairs with pointed and rounded toes designed for Maharanis; they're comfortable even to my feet, which are more accustomed to sandals. I would love a couple of pairs for myself and Shabbir and I work out a design that incorporates soft leather and embroidery, and yet is not too expensive. We reduce the embroidery to just a beige silk rosette to lower the cost and then we discuss the price. 'I won't over-charge you, but I won't undercharge either,' says Shabbir. 'Leave the price to me.'

It is growing dark now, and the bazaar is closing. Most of the homes I pass as I head back to my hotel are lit by the decidedly unatmospheric glare of electricity-saving neon. Televisions blare at full volume and children and adults are firmly glued to the screens. I recall how television is changing the fabric of life even in our little village of Patan. With the introduction of late-night movies, families tend to sleep only when the films end, whereas before they had television they would have been asleep soon after sundown. As a result, few people are able to wake with the dawn any more. The day starts late, children don't finish their homework and the advertisements introduce 'needs' that cannot always be fulfilled.

Maharaja Gaj Singh's secretary shows me into a small, intimate room with a pleasant mix of comfortable sofas and elegant period furniture. There are family portraits on the walls, photo-graphs in silver frames, cabinets with glass curios, porcelain figurines and large arrangements of fresh flowers.

A miniature dachshund bounds into the room with a tinkling of tiny bells, followed by an attendant who ushers me into the next room. Gaj Singh II, thirty-ninth Maharaja of Jodhpur, is a handsome man whose neatly trimmed moustache and matching sideburns are just beginning to grey. He wears the region's distinctive jodhpurs, a short tunic-like *kurta*, a close-fitting waistcoat in textured cotton and embroidered *jootis*. But what strikes me most is his gentle dignity; I have no difficulty falling into the traditional form of address and instinctively call him Bapji, father.

The Maharaja returned to Jodhpur in 1970 to a tumultuous welcome after a long liberal education in England. 'It was the ultimate statement of continuity,' he says, 'of expectation from that continuity. But I had nothing to offer in terms of power, so it was even more touching.' He hastens to qualify his statement. 'The respect is not for myself, but for what I represent. The people don't see me as an individual but as a symbol of Jodhpur, of a past in which they have pride.' I like his self-deprecation, and sympathise with this man, who inherited responsibility and commitment without the means to fulfil them.

We speak about his children, a daughter and a son. 'They are almost adults now. They have been fortunate to have the best of both worlds: an early education in India and then school followed by college in England. They have confidence in themselves and know that they belong to a secure, happy family with an old tradition. They also realise that they have a responsibility to that tradition, a responsibility that they must accept because they have benefited from it.'

I refer to the abolition of the privy purse and the stripping of titles and privileges. 'It was not just a question of money,' he says. 'It was more the loss of prestige. One day we were looked up to, and suddenly in the new socialistic system we were looked down on. We had visible assets, highly visible assets, but no income. And the whole system was opposed to us. History was distorted to justify that opposition, and we were written off as a tyrannical feudal order. All the real contributions we made were swept under the carpet. But the people did not forget.'

During the first democratic elections of free India, Bapji's father, Maharaja Hanumant Singhji, put up forty-five candidates, of whom forty-one won their election. 'It was said,' laughs Bapji, 'that if my father put up a donkey against the Congress candidate, it would win.'

The socialism of the 1970s, Bapji explains, affected the conservation effort, as there was a feeling that everything old must be left behind. It became fashionable to dismiss conservation as elitist and backward looking, and many forts and palaces crumbled into oblivion as a result.

'Weren't some palaces converted into government offices, schools and hospitals?' I ask.

'Putting the old buildings to new use was a good idea of course,' says Bapji, 'except that the conversions were unplanned, and continuing shortages of funds turned grand buildings into depressing dumps filled with battered desks and chairs and ragged stacks of files.

'Everybody realises,' he continues thoughtfully, 'that conservation cannot be the responsibility of the government alone; it cannot possibly do everything. Everyone has to do more.'

Bapji is talking my language: I have long been an advocate of corporate responsibility and the increasing role that industry must play in matters such as conservation, art and sport. But there are problems with privately owned palaces too. Hotels are one solution, but when palaces are converted into hotels, there remains the problem of accessibility for the local people.

'We have partially solved the problem at Jodhpur's Umaid Bhavan Palace by converting several public rooms into a museum which is enormously popular among the local people.' Bapji sighs deeply. 'But a museum's income is small compared to the costs of maintenance and conservation. There is so much to do and so little funding.'

Raja Bhupat Singh is an expert on the Marwari horses used by Rajputs for centuries. We sit talking in his small front room; the curtains are patterned with horses, there are pictures of horses on the walls, statues of horses on the mantelpiece and a saddle in one corner – even the cushion I am sitting on has horses embroidered on it.

'When the Rathores came to Marwar,' Raja Bhupat explains, 'they bred a special horse that could survive in this inhospitable land. It couldn't be a big horse because food was in short supply, yet it had to be able to carry a man in full armour for a whole day.'

As he talks, he moves to the window and looks out distractedly. I cough to remind him that I am still in the room. 'The horse had to have long legs, to distance its body from the hot sand,' he continues. 'It was also essential that it had stamina because the Rajputs believed in hand-to-hand fighting, exhausting for men but also for horses. Speed was not so important, because it was shameful to run.'

There is a clattering on the drive and a beautiful piebald horse prances by. Raja Bhupat dashes outside and pats and talks to the animal animatedly. He turns to me beaming, and continues on his pet subject.

'Since a Marwari horse was essentially bred for battle, two things were important: first, that it should present as small a target as possible; and second, that it should be highly manoeuvrable.'

He pats the horse's rear, and strokes the sweeping curve of its specially bred sickle hock, designed to reduce the horse's size while enabling it to jump from almost a standing position. He draws my attention to the horse's beautifully arched neck, carefully bred to a curve to avoid injury by the sword.

'Notice the ears,' he urges, 'see how they are placed close to the centre of the head, curving inwards and almost touching. They allow the warrior rider to brandish his sword without fear of injuring his horse. In comparison, the straight ears of the thoroughbred look like the ears of a mule.'

Until now, I had only seen horses like this in miniature paintings, and had always attributed the impossibly arched neck, curving ears and lovely lines of the hock to the artist's fancy.

'Rajput men love their horses dearly, but all Rajput ladies curse them,' says Raja Bhupat. 'My late wife used to complain that she would try everything to wake me, but was always unsuccessful. "But a neigh from the stables, and you are instantly awake." '

Raja Bhupat steps back, hands on his hips, regarding his horse with joy. 'Thoroughbreds cannot take our terrain or our sun. Only our Marwari horses can survive in the desert. Our lives have depended on them.'

CHAPTER 7
BIKANER

ATE ONE afternoon, I decide on an impulse to take a drive into the countryside. I am not a city person and, much as I enjoy Jodhpur, I feel stifled. I ask Udai Singh to take the same road I had been on with Mr Tak, and a group of women sitting by the side of the road wave to us to stop. They are Rabaris, I gather from the white bangles one wears up to her armpit, and they want a lift home.

The three women, a mother around my age and her two daughters, hop happily into the car and squeeze onto the back seat together. The girls are around sixteen and eighteen, with glowing, flawless skins. They bounce excitedly on the seat, talking and giggling in shrill, high voices.

'They have never sat in any vehicle before,' Tungli, their mother, apologises, 'not even a bus.'

Tungli's eyes contain all the browns of the earth: the sand, the camel, the gazelle, the fox. In addition to her arm bracelets, four sets of silver earrings dangle from her stretched ear lobes. Tattoo marks in elaborate designs that simulate jewellery are worked onto her wrists and the backs of her hands. What especially catches my fancy are the gold motifs embedded into her few remaining teeth.

I admire her ornaments and she smiles in pleasure. A bond forms between us that bridges the huge gap that separates our lives. We are simply two women who like each other, and would like to know more about the other's life. Her daughters are both married but they do not yet live with their husbands; that is why they don't wear the white bangles up to the armpit like their mother.

'We like to keep our daughters with us for as long as possible,' Tungli says. 'There is so much work to do and it all falls on us women. The men are away herding sheep for eight months of the year.'

The family have five goats, about twenty camels and 'six twenties' of sheep. I am charmed by Tungli's ability to compensate for her ignorance of larger numbers, a skill that I'm sure she applies with competence to the managing of her family's affairs. I think about the difference between intelligence and literacy: how arrogant it is to assume that a woman who cannot write her name lacks intelligence!

Since the men are away for most of the year, Tungli copes entirely on her own. She sows and harvests the family's fields, and after putting aside enough to see the family through the year, markets the surplus produce. She deals with rapacious officials and lecherous upper-caste men who eye her daughters.

When we stop at their village, the girls get out of the car with many flounces and flourishes for the benefit of an audience of jabbering children, who follow us to Tungli's hut, trying out their English, asking for pens and tugging at my clothing. I am mildly irritated until I realise that just as I am curious about their lives, so they are curious about mine.

Tungli's hut is round with a conical thatched roof, and sits in a small compound surrounded by a low mud wall. There are no windows, and the hut is thus insulated from Marwar's extreme climate. There is no chimney either, but the smoke from the wood fire that Tungli lights to make us a cup of tea escapes through chinks in the thatch.

We chat over a cup of the hot sweet liquid, made faintly pungent by the addition of goat's milk. I ask Tungli if she has ever accompanied her husband on the annual migration. She used to, she tells me, but the situation has become difficult now. There are conflicts with farmers who now regard the Rabaris with antipathy; previously they would pay them to graze their herds in fallow fields because of the animals' rich droppings. There is also often trouble with the forestry department, which forbids entry into protected areas. And then there is harassment from government officials, because Rabaris now have to obtain permits to enter different states and pay a fee based on the size of their herd. The herdsmen frequently fudge their numbers and so there is more trouble.

'As a result of the many difficulties in migration,' she says, 'we have begun to realise that the old ways will soon cease altogether. So it is important that our children go to school, to prepare them for a different life. Which brings added importance to us women staying at home.'

Tungli has anticipated the future: Rabari men will probably get jobs with the Camel Corps of the Border Security force. They are expert trackers, able to recognise and track individual animals by their hoof prints, and are also skilled rural vets. I think with sorrow of the inevitable cessation of their nomadism, which will change Rabari lifestyles and dilute their identity for ever. I am reminded of the changes that I have constantly encountered in Rajasthan, of vanishing lifestyles that endured for centuries, and I fear the consequences of the settling of these people: more pressure on existing land, more unemployment, more frustration. The price of progress.

The next day, we leave Jodhpur before dawn to drive through the flat expanse of Marusthali – the region of the dead. I am filled with anticipation as we head towards Rajasthan's desert heart at last. Marusthali's low dunes are part of the great Thar Desert, the arid mass of shifting sands that covers over half of the state and is kept in check by the Aravalli hills. The annual rainfall here is less than three hundred millimetres; wells are few and the sun is merciless. It occurs to me that this is the time of day when the great caravans would have been on the move, trying to cover as much ground as possible before the relentless sun rose high in the sky.

An unexpected wind stirs the sand, making it swirl and rise up like a great corkscrew. I eagerly lower my window, wanting to participate in this great spectacle. I ask Udai Singh to stop and, to his surprise, I get out of the car. The mauling wind whips the trees, making them writhe and cavort like dervishes. The cloud of sand flattens out and spreads like a living, suffocating blanket. It gets into my eyes and ears, beneath my nails and into my mouth. But although I have the option of an insulated car, I prefer for the moment to stand outside in the howling wind, thinking of what it must have been like to travel through this great convulsion of earth and sky.

The sun rises behind the veil of sand and slowly the desert's harshness is softened by a radiating tinge of pink. Surrounded by this unearthly incandescence, I feel strengthened and inspired, and although my participation is peripheral, I begin to appreciate the beauty that the nomads I have met have all struggled to describe.

Suddenly, the wind dies down and the storm passes. I can see the great cloud of sand billowing towards the horizon, travelling all the time. I wonder how long it will take to reach Delhi and whether the plantations of my childhood will arrest its inexorable passage. I shake myself like a wet dog to dislodge particles of sand, and when I look around, I realise that I am not in the middle of a sandy desert after all, but on a rocky plain covered in olive-coloured shrubs. The desert of my imaginings continues to elude me.

As we approach the town of Nagaur, there are increasing numbers of red chilli stalls along the roadside. 'There are many different kinds of chillies,' Udai tells me. 'The variety often differs from village to village.'

211

We stop to investigate, and inhale the sharp, nose-tickling aromas. There are thin chillies and fat ones, long and short ones, thick-skinned and thin-skinned ones, dark red and pink ones. Each has its individual flavour and qualities: 'The cognoscenti can tell the difference,' Udai assures me.

Chillies induce perspiration and therefore cool the body. They also zip up boring, repetitive fare, but since they are a dominant flavour, they are used sparingly in more sophisticated cuisine. For the poor, however, they are a staple; a chutney of garlic and red chillies is often the only accompaniment to a farmer's *rotis*. Their pungency helps a little food go a long way, and also induces the sensation of a full stomach.

We drive on through narrow streets so crowded with shops and houses that we somehow miss the huge gateway to Nagaur's fort, crammed between the innumerable little businesses which have been built into its massive walls. At the office inside the gate, the manager of the fort voices his concern at these growing encroachments: the moat and walls have been virtually obliterated by new construction.

His wife, Preeti, joins in the conversation. 'Today,' she says, 'the fort is threatened not by mighty armies, nor the ravages of plundering conquerors, but by the mundane yet more sinister pressure of uncontrolled urban growth.'

She looks like any other small-town Rajput lady, but as she talks I notice that her speech is graceful and her observations perceptive. 'The problem is that people no longer identify with the fort. Unlike Jodhpur's Meherangarh, Ahhichatragarh has not been occupied for years, and so it is no longer a symbol of pride.

212

History too has played its part, as the fort changed hands with bewildering rapidity.'

Preeti holds a Master's degree in medieval Rajput history and was commissioned by Monty's museum trust to work on the conservation of Ahhichatragarh fort. 'I was terribly nervous,' she says frankly. 'I had never stepped out of my home, let alone travelled to do research.'

It is difficult to appreciate the enormous courage it must have taken for Preeti to accept the commission, given her obviously conservative upbringing. She is now an expert on Ahhichatragarh, which she tells me was first fortified in the fourth century AD. Nagaur lay along the route to Delhi, and was an oasis for both travellers and traders in a region of such hostile desolation.

'It has been referred to as a shuttlecock,' she smiles, 'passed from hand to hand in the cycle of conquest and defeat that ended in the Moghul period when it became an outpost of Marwar.'

We wander through the fort's palaces and pavilions, deserted today but richly peopled by the past. The conversations, emotions and pleasures of the former inhabitants linger like perfume in the empty chambers.

Preeti shows me a network of air ducts that supplied cooled air to the innermost rooms. We walk on through rooms where frescoes jolt the senses with their breathtaking grace. Water channels chiselled in fish-scale patterns ripple down walls and disappear beneath the floor to emerge again in silent spouts, from which water would once have cascaded in handfuls of flung diamonds. The cooling potential and aesthetic possibilities of every precious drop were exploited to the hilt.

Gardens surround the palace's courtyards and balconies in a delicate counterpoise of space and mass. The balconies are carefully positioned to catch the smallest breeze, and the air is further cooled by the large pools of water and fountains that intersect the gardens. Preeti describes the complex water system and ingenious engineering which made all this possible. The technical competence of her discourse is impressive. But what she misses, or at least does not say, is that pleasure and indulgent fantasy are the essence of Nagaur.

A camel festival is in progress when I arrive in Bikaner, and the town is crowded with camel enthusiasts. I have always loved camels. I admire their snooty, mildly amused expressions, their long eyelashes and their soft lower lip. I have two of my own at home: a skittish and very leggy six-month-old baby and her mother, who is one of the most beautiful camels I have ever seen, with huge, dark, gentle eyes, impossibly curling eyelashes, the most elegantly arched neck and an intelligent manner of listening to you by flicking her ears forward. The little one is called Masti, mischief, but as a diminutive name was clearly inappropriate for her mother, we named that lovely and gracious lady Jehanara Begum. The camels had been reared by nomadic Rabari herds-men from the desert around Jodhpur, and as a result were essentially feral when Ajit gave them to me for my birthday; they had never been stall fed, nor had they ever been tethered.

I dream that night of Masti and Jehanara in a confused collage

214

of homesick memories and, with them very much in mind, head off next morning for the local parade ground to learn, I hope, the finer points of camel appreciation. A marquee along one side overlooks a large, dusty open space where dozens of camels are milling around, awaiting the start of the milking competition.

'The she camel is the cow of the desert,' the master of ceremonies announces over the loud speaker. 'Camel milk is rich in vitamin C and highly nutritious, and although it has a slightly salty taste, it is most pleasant and very good for one.' As much as I love camels, I have difficulty accepting the idea of drinking their milk.

Seven female camels are led to the front of the viewing area, each with a calf which begins to suckle but is dragged away when a piercing whistle signals the beginning of the competition. The milkers start work, with serious and continued competition from the calves. There is confused shouting and swearing, pushing and pulling, until the whistle blows again, followed by repeated injunctions to stop milking. But many of the contestants continue milking while they can, like school children in an exam trying to write another couple of words after the finishing bell. And they have several complaints. 'I started late,' exclaims one; 'My container fell to the ground and I had to begin all over again,' complains another.

While the judges are making up their minds, besieged by clamouring contestants, more camels are lining up to compete in the category for the best decorations; one camel indicates his disapproval of the entire proceedings by spewing out his soft palate at his admiring audience. This competition is designed to promote traditional handmade adornments, testimony to continuing folk art skills that are expressions of everyday life and the local enjoyment of colour and ornament. The announcer is trying to make himself heard over the din: 'It is said that when the camel is decorated the animal is happy. It walks tall and proudly.'

I am particularly interested in this event as I want to buy some jewellery for my own camels – a *ghorband* perhaps, an elaborate neckpiece traditionally festooned with shells, beads and silk tassels. One of the camels is wearing a *ghorband* made of the plastic counters used in casinos. I find it hard to resist the many other accoutrements on display: fine hand-tooled saddles, embroidered saddle cloths embellished with mirrors and shells, and knee and ankle bands adorned with silk tassels and tiny bells.

More camels parade past, and this time the judges take note of the animals' decorative shearing. Their thick winter coats have been clipped to re-create the intricate floral and geometric motifs that I have seen in painting and sculpture, and which have now been brought into high relief on these live canvases.

Next on the agenda is judging the way the camels walk – a serious consideration if you ride one often. The announcer informs us that 'The gait should be so smooth that even if you were to carry a full container of milk on the camel's back, not a drop would spill.'

Bhawal Khan, a breeder of considerable repute, wears a silver medal on a silver cord around his neck. 'I won it last year,' he says, touching it like a talisman. 'I was awarded first prize for the best dancing camel.'

He tells me how, according to legend, camels were created.

'It all began with bulls,' he says. 'Shiva created his bull, Nandi, with a fifth leg on its neck – that is why deformed cows are always worshipped. His consort, Parvati, decided she too wanted an animal for herself and fashioned a funny-looking animal out of the sand. Shiva laughed at its long legs and neck: "It's too stupid to breathe life into," he said. But Parvati insisted, so Shiva took Nandi's fifth leg and attached it to the camel's back; then he brought the sand animal to life. The word camel comes from the Sanskrit *kreluk*, which means "throw away legs".'

I am enchanted by this apt description of a running camel, for I have often laughed when watching Masti and Jehanara's ridiculous lack of control over their legs when running.

A performance of the famous Bhavai dance by ten-year-old Swati Khatri provides a short break from camels. The little girl dances balancing a *matka* on her head while her small feet grip the edges of a large brass plate, which she moves in time to the percussion, her hands simultaneously weaving delicate patterns. She climbs onto four Coca-Cola bottles, two under each foot, and proceeds to dance on them. The spectators begin to clap in time to the music. Without faltering, she steps off the bottles and onto a pile of broken glass, treading on it to the accompanying music and the tinkle of breaking glass. The audience applauds again and again. A bed of nails is her next platform and the finale comes as Swati dances along the thin edge of a sword. Although the blade must be blunt, her sense of balance, which is also the key to dancing on the glass, is incredible.

My moustachioed neighbour turns out to be a friend of Swati's family who has come along for moral support. 'She started learning only about four years ago,' he tells me. He calls out to Swati, who comes up to him and proceeds to talk to me with complete self-assurance.

'Don't your feet hurt?' I ask.

'Not at all,' she replies, slipping off her sandals and showing me her little feet, which have been painted with a red cosmetic to draw attention to their movements. Swati has soft baby feet without a trace of a callus.

'What about school?' I ask.

'I am in the sixth standard,' she says in her high, piping voice, 'and I do well in my studies. My favourite subject is maths.'

'And what do you want to be when you grow up?' I ask indulgently, expecting to hear dreams about Hindi films, professional dancing and so on.

She flips back her hair and her pudgy face becomes serious, 'I will sit for the Indian Administrative Exam and do very well and then I will become a Collector.'

A folk music performance takes place that evening in a clearing in front of the imposing Junagarh, the old palace. I look up at the traceried windows which form the musicians' backdrop. They would have been illuminated from within in times gone by, shining out into the night, and in the rooms behind them, oil lamps flickering in carved alcoves would have led the way to passion and intrigue.

The desert is famous for its music, which in many remote

hamlets was the primary form of entertainment. Musical instruments were developed by those nomads who lived the loneliest of lives, and were refined by itinerant entertainers whose livelihood was music.

A group with several sets of percussion, string and wind instruments takes the stage. Some are purely folk instruments, others have been modified by the more sophisticated influences of the imperial Moghul court at Delhi. The main drum beat is particularly emphatic, like a giant heart pulsing. The drummer's fingers create a range of effects: the roar of a fighting army, the rustling of leaves and the ripple of water.

The strings wail and the wind instruments moan in sensual rhythms as the musicians create a picture of a shepherd huddled over a fire, playing his flute to keep himself awake as he watches over his flock in the cold night, the clear notes hanging like icicles in the dry desert air.

I am back at Junagarh the next morning completely unprepared for the flamboyant beauty of its palaces. I thought I had already seen all Rajasthan had to offer – palace after beautiful palace – but nothing has prepared me for this. The decorative impulse that I have encountered throughout the state reaches a mighty crescendo here: walls and ceilings are painted, lacquered and gilded, decorated with mosaics, etched glass and inlaid mirrors. It invokes a delightful sense of the abandoned enjoyment of painter and patron, an unabashed revelling in glitter and ostentation, and although the workmanship is superb, I am reminded most of a child let loose with a box of crayons.

My favourite room is Badal Mahal, where stylised clouds drift across blue walls, interspersed with brilliant yellow lightning and streaking rain. Shivshankar Saini, a guide from the tourist office, points out a concealed water tank. When the sun blazed outside Badal Mahal, the royal inhabitants enjoyed the luxury of simulated rain.

When I try to peer through the intricately traceried windows I'd been admiring the night before, I find it frustratingly difficult to get a clear view. For the first time I can truly empathise with the generations of women who had no option but to have their field of vision so restricted.

Saini takes me through endless painted rooms and up high, narrow staircases to Hawa Mahal, palace of the clouds. The chamber is patterned with gilded paintings, as well as with blue Delft and Chinese tiles, procured from the caravans that were the source of much of Bikaner's wealth. Saini draws my attention to mirrors on the ceiling, placed so that the Maharaja could see almost every corner of the fort from his bed. I also suspect they were thus placed so that he could view himself and the lady of his choice in the languorous positions of love, but I keep the thought to myself.

Back on the ground floor, weapons are displayed in room after room. Traditional Rajput arms, each a piece of art, are juxtaposed with light machine guns from World War I and a fifty-kilo elephant gun that used five kilos of powder.

Pride of place goes to the huge double-edged sword of

Rajkumar Padam Singh. 'With this sword that few can lift,' says thin, bespectacled Saini, 'Padam Singh left a dent on a sandstone pillar at Agra when he cut down his brother's murderer in front of Emperor Aurangzeb.' Such weapons are icons to the Rajputs, and their stories legitimise and reinforce the magnificent madness that sustained and inspired them.

Carved red sandstone smothers every surface in Maharaja Ganga Singh's enormous audience hall. Ganga Singh was a giant of a man, both physically and intellectually; he was one of the most outstanding Indian princes of the twentieth century. When he ascended the throne in 1898, aged eighteen, a famine was devastating Bikaner; the young Maharaja travelled by camel from village to village and saw hundreds die of starvation. From this dreadful initiation grew a dream: to bring water to the desert. His obsession resulted in the Ganga Canal, commissioned in 1927; desert-bound Bikaner became the granary of Rajasthan. In recent years, Ganga Singh's concept has been expanded beyond his imaginings to the Great Rajasthan Canal, which it is hoped will bring similar benefits to Jaisalmer.

Unfortunately, I've missed the fire dance for which Bikaner is famous. The dancers are members of the Siddh Naths, a religious sect whose incredible austerities are said to give them supernatural powers. The fire dance is both a spectacular feat of endurance and a manifestation of this power.

I have heard strange stories about the Siddh Naths. Their cult is very ancient and has been associated with various occult practices. They performed miracles and attracted hordes of followers; they also foretold the future and wielded enormous temporal power through Rajas who were their devotees.

I discover that one of the secular heads of the cult lives in town and make an appointment to meet him. When I arrive at his home in a small dusty lane, I interrupt the women of the family at their morning meal. In most conservative families men still eat first, a convention that had a practical basis since it was the woman's role to make the *rotis*: each man would eat at least four, and they had to be fresh, so the women were kept busy until the men had finished.

Sat Nath, the patriarch of the family, occupies a small room on the second floor of the house. A single bed and rows of book shelves are the only furniture; a folding chair has been set up for me. The old man sits cross-legged on his bed, wrapped in a blanket; he is a big man, physically powerful, with enormous hands. With him is his grandson, Yashpal, a bright-eyed ten-year-old.

'He too is a fire dancer, like myself,' says the old man. 'I used to be very good. I also developed some choreography for the dance to make it look more spectacular.'

The fire dance, according to Sat Nath, is performed only by those who have stilled the mind and achieved various powers, including a purity that protects them from fire. The lore of the Siddh Naths is replete with stories of the supernatural prowess of adepts who emerged unscathed from pits of flame, escaped from barred prisons and performed other feats to demonstrate the dominance of mind and the protection of the gods. Today's fire dance is a pale imitation of the real thing.

The children of the Siddh Naths are taught the technique from a very early age. 'The feet must be kept firm and tight, and only the soles should be in contact with the coals. Fire dancing is really a question of experience, balance and complete concentration. You must tread lightly on the fire, and it is essential that the feet be kept in constant motion. Even when the dancer is stationary, his feet must keep moving, even imperceptibly.'

A ring of wet soil is laid around the fire and kept damp. The dancers walk around the fire on this wet earth before treading on the fire, and the cold seeps deep into their bones to help them withstand the heat. On the opposite side of the fire hangs a pink flag with peacock feathers tied to it. 'We focus on this when we cross the embers,' the old man tells me.

The dancers are extremely careful about what they eat. All their food is cooked in the purest ghee, and they eat only the best quality vegetables and lentils. On the day of the dance they eat only a lentil *halwa* – food which gives them strength and contains nothing that could even minutely disrupt their equilibrium.

During the fire dance, the dancers sing songs based on mantras that induce a heightened state of being, and drums beat for added courage. Most dancers walk across the fire in a quick series of steps, but there are some who are able to stand for long periods among the flames. 'Even we are astonished,' Sat Nath says with reverence, 'we have to acknowledge that there is something extra at work. Something from the old days, some special power.'

Bikaner is home to the largest wholesale wool market in the country – indeed, in Asia. A brand-new enclave of warehouses and offices has recently replaced the old makeshift stalls, but it feels rather desolate: row upon row of identical utilitarian boxes, surrounded by tired saplings. I feel sorry for the Rabari herdsmen who have to come to this drab place to sell their wool.

A watchman at one of the few warehouses with any sign of life explains the current lack of activity. 'It's the off season; the sheep won't be sheared for another couple of weeks yet, so business is slow. During peak season the noise and the bustle are something to be seen. There are over a hundred and fifty warehouses, all crowded. Rabaris arrive with their wool, buyers congregate and auctions are held several times a day.'

Some Rabaris from warmer parts have already sheared their sheep and are here to sell the wool. Their white *dhotis* and bright turbans contrast sharply with the undistinguished trousers and shirts of the more urbanised buyers. They join in our conversation, made curious by the unusual presence of a woman.

The market deals with over a hundred and twenty-five thousand kilograms of wool every day, but most of the wool is fairly coarse and used mainly by the carpet industry. Indian wool production is low compared to demand and over seventy per cent of the wool for even the carpet industry is imported from Australia.

'So there is plenty of scope for expansion of the industry,' I remark, 'more sheep, better wool-bearing breeds, and so on.'

'We already have a problem with pastures,' says one of the Rabaris, chewing his *paan* noisily, 'so how can we increase the number of our herds? The famous Rajasthan Canal, that everyone is so grateful for, will destroy graziers and merchants alike. Every year hundreds, even thousands, of hectares of prime pasture is converted to agricultural use.'

Another of the Rabaris, an older man with a strong face, speaks with authority. 'Already we have to travel the country in search of good grass for our herds. But at least we were able to come home during the rainy months and could graze our sheep in the local pastures. Now this too will be just a memory.'

'What about stall feeding?' I ask.

'It's a strange thing,' he muses, rubbing the stubble on his chin, 'but for a sheep to produce good-quality and abundant wool it must walk. At least ten kilometres every day.'

'As they eat, so is their wool,' says another Rabari, bending to pick up a handful of matted wool. 'If they eat dry grass, the wool is white like this. Green grass produces wool with a yellow tinge.'

An auction is about to commence in a warehouse across the road, and I follow the crowd into a courtyard. The auctioneer fixes a base price with the Rabaris, who are spreading their wool in big heaps on the ground, and gestures to the buyers to begin. Bidding is brisk and the price inches up.

But mutton, not wool, is the Rabaris' main source of income. 'The wool barely pays for our shoes,' says one of the younger Rabaris, with a grin.

Shivshankar Saini drives with me to Deshnok, thirty kilometres south of Bikaner and home to the famous temple of Karni Mata, a powerful local manifestation of the goddess Durga. Outside the temple, which is swarming with scores of holy rats known as *kaaba*, Saini introduces me to Dharmraj, a gnarled old man in a grimy *dhoti* and an army-surplus overcoat, who unfolds himself from his seat in the sun to greet us.

Dharmraj is a direct descendant of Karni Mata, Saini explains. 'As evil grows, the *devi* becomes incarnate,' Dharmraj says, with natural dramatic instinct. 'This region resonates with the special power of the goddess. We believe that most Rajput goddesses are manifestations of her.'

But before telling me more about Karni Mata and her rodent acolytes, he insists that I first understand the origin of the *charans*, the bards among whom she was born.

'The Rajputs,' he says in a loud, strong voice, 'were losing the urge to fight. And if the Rajput cannot fight, he cannot live. So Lord Shiva created us *charans* to urge them on to greater and greater deeds of valour. And his consort, the goddess, promised that she would repeatedly be reborn among us.' He leans back against the old tree. 'We are *deva putra*, born of the gods.'

Dharmraj reaches into the voluminous pockets of his overcoat for a packet of *bidi*, selects one and lights it. 'There has always been a *charan* in every Rajput court, to show the king the way. We never put our hand out for money, we earned it with our tongues. The *charan* and the Rajput were as inseparable as body and soul. We were not just wandering minstrels, but politicians, warriors and poets.'

It was among these people, tending her herds, that Karni Mata grew up. 'All the cattle you see in this region are descended from the *devi*'s herds,' Dharmraj says. 'She set aside an area of three square kilometres exclusively for the cows. It is sinful to cultivate these lands or to cut a single tree from them, for they are the sacred property of the goddess.'

Karni Mata was born in the fourteenth century, and as she grew up she began to perform miracles. When her nephew died, she went to the nether world to plead with Yamraj, god of death, for the life of the boy. She promised that she would never bother Yamraj again; in future, she would look after her own. 'Their souls will not add to your burden,' she promised, 'and when my descendants die they shall become *kaaba*, sacred rats, for one lifetime and be reborn again as *charans*.'

'So you see, all these rats are actually my relatives,' Dharmraj says as he puffs on his *bidi*. 'Now you should visit the temple. Pay particular attention to the sanctum; it was built by the goddess herself of just stone and mud. She didn't even permit the use of cow dung to bind the mortar, as she believed that all dung should be preserved to use as fuel, thus saving trees.'

We enter the courtyard, which is roofed with wire mesh to protect the *kaaba* from predators. I have had to remove my shoes, and am grateful for the thick socks that I remembered to put on in the morning. The *kaaba* are everywhere. My skin crawls as one scurries over my feet and Saini advises me to shuffle to avoid the dreadful sin of stepping on one. I stifle my squeamishness as I shuffle to the sanctum, where my attempts to focus on the shrine are distracted by the *kaaba* which are crawling everywhere, lapping at a large pot of milk and devouring the specially made *halwa* which is offered to the *kaaba* in large quantities by devotees.

'It is important to remember that it is Karni Mata who is worshipped here,' Saini says, 'not the *kaaba*. The temple is just a sanctuary for them.'

Dharmraj, who had been praying at the shrine, joins us again and insists that I perform a circumambulation of the sanctum. I protest weakly and to no effect, so we shuffle along the ritual path into dark corridors infested with twittering *kaaba*. Little rat holes have been carefully built into the skirting of all the walls.

'Be careful,' Dharmraj says, as I leap up to avoid a particularly persistent *kaaba*, 'that may be my grandfather.'

CHAPTER 8
JAISALMER

THE ROAD to Jaisalmer is ruler straight. I can see for miles. The only sign of habitation is the occasional clutch of round huts; I can imagine the wind whipping the dust around them in summer. Cows amble across the flatness and pause to graze. In the far distance a woman walks to her village, her pink *odhni* streaming in the wind against the patchwork landscape of beiges and browns.

I have decided to make a short detour to visit Khichan, and we follow the signs directing us off the main road. The quiet village is full of abandoned but well-maintained *havelis*, built of richly carved red sandstone, but I have come to see the demoiselle cranes that fly here all the way from the steppes of Eurasia and Mongolia. The flocks arrive in large, dark clouds every year towards the last week of August, just after the monsoon rains have ceased, and return to their breeding grounds towards the end of March.

Prakash Jain is one of the local enthusiasts who look after the birds' needs. We manage to locate his house, which is tucked behind an ornate *haveli*, and he takes me to the pen on the outskirts of the village where the cranes are fed.

We are just in time for the evening feeding. The huge, sandy pen is packed with thousands of cranes, pecking at the grain strewn there for them by the villagers. The birds' red and grey plumage gleams in the evening light and their black chest feathers stand out like neckties. I am warned to walk very slowly, not to point and only to look at the birds out of the corner of my eye.

'They are vigilant and shy,' Prakash explains apologetically. 'Passing camel carts do not disturb them, but if they spot a stranger a single alarm call is enough to make the whole lot take off.'

Sparrows, peacocks, crows, pigeons and chickens also partake of the meal while more flocks of cranes circle overhead waiting for the next sitting. Some of the earlier arrivals take off clumsily, due to the lack of space in the enclosure, but in a disciplined order. They head for the dunes on the other side of the feeding pen, where dinner is rounded off by seeds and small crumbs of lime. I watch entranced.

The people of Khichan have been feeding the cranes for over a hundred years. Later, at Prakash Jain's house, he propounds a surprising theory as to why this is so. 'It originates in astrology,' he announces, 'not just humane practices. The malefic planet Rahu enters everyone's horoscope at one time or another, and the colour associated with the planet is a greyish red, the colour of the rock pigeon and the demoiselle crane. So in order to placate Rahu, people have always fed these two species.'

Prakash's interest in astrology led to his current activities as a one-man marriage bureau for Jains. Men and women send him their horoscopes and fill in the forms he has developed, listing their personal details as well as the qualities they desire in their marriage partners. Prakash tallies the horoscopes, chooses a selection of appropriate spouses and mails back the details.

'I do it because I enjoy the stimulation of my intellect,' he says. 'It's my hobby, not my business. I charge only postage.'

According to Prakash, *karak lagan*, the Cancer ascendant in the horoscope, is one of the main problems in marriage: it leads to the untimely death of the other partner. Jawaharlal Nehru, Indira Gandhi, the god king Rama and the ancient emperor Ashoka all had a Cancer ascendant, and all of them lost their spouses. Prakash discovered that he too had a Cancer ascendant, and sure enough his wife died young.

I tell Prakash that I haven't had my horoscope made because I don't want to know what will happen in the future. This angers him, and he shouts at me: 'You have come with your driver to my house. If you felt like this, why did you plan your trip? Why did you not just leave your house without any plan or direction? Then you would have come here only if your path fell this way. If you are willing to plan the superficial details of your life, then how can you say you don't want to know what will happen in the future?'

Pemaram is short and stringy with an overgrown white moustache. He is a weaver and lives with his five sons in the little hamlet we've stopped at on the main road to Jaisalmer. Like so many hand-loom weavers all over the country, he saw both his craft and his livelihood languishing some years ago; times had changed but he couldn't understand the new demands of his market. Then a voluntary social work group stepped in with design ideas and marketing strategies. Pemaram's looms started clattering again and haven't stopped since.

We walk together into his compound, where there are four small houses: one for the looms, two for his married sons, and one for Pemaram, his wife and their unmarried children. In this arrangement the family gains security and support from each other, yet retains some privacy. But there are drawbacks to this proximity; when one of the sons appears wearing terry-towelling trousers and shirt, Pemaram launches into what must be a familiar tirade against the young man's modern clothing.

Bhagwanlal, who wears the offending garments, protests, 'They are more convenient.'

'More constricting,' his father retorts.

'More in keeping with the times than your *dhoti*.'

'Whoever saw a weaver of cotton wearing terry?' Pemaram asks me in disgust.

The looms are simple and homemade, consisting of two beams held in place by wooden posts fixed into the ground. The old man sits on the floor with his legs in a pit dug under the loom; he works the wooden beam, deftly sending the shuttles spinning through the threads as he weaves intricate patterns of red, yellow and white on a black background. His fingers fly and the fabric grows inch by inch.

'The big advantage of our work is that we can weave at any

time we like,' says Pemaram. 'There is no rigid demarcation between work and leisure. And when we are doing simpler work, our wives and children often sit around and we chat.'

Pemaram and his sons used to weave plain, natural-coloured cotton goods but they were taught to incorporate colours and designs by the social work group. The new products sell better and the family can charge higher prices for them.

'It's a good life,' Pemaram says with satisfaction. 'I am no-one's slave. I don't have to answer to anybody. And there is also a sense of personal responsibility: the more I work, the more money I make for myself and my family.'

All the boys have been to school. 'Education,' Pemaram says, 'has given us the edge that we need. The advantage is tremendous. We are better able to cope with the outside world.'

'Some of the work we do is incredibly painstaking,' Bhagwanlal interjects. 'Once I got fed up with it all and I gave up weaving and got a job driving a tractor. But at the end of the day, I felt sort of empty, drab. There was none of the satisfaction that we get in weaving. It's an aesthetic satisfaction that we don't even realise we are receiving.'

Bhagwanlal is married and has three children. 'That is my father's grandson,' he says, indicating a child with a frilled bonnet and kohled eyes. 'He is the weaver of the future.'

A chinkara bounds across the road to Jaisalmer, its hooves clicking on the tarmac. The wilderness and its creatures are alive and well because the sand has been smothered in rich plantations of tall grass. The desert has been contained, and Ajit's experience of sand obliterating the road to Jaisalmer is history.

We drive briefly through Akal, the fossil park that reinforces the theory that great forests once stretched across this land. Stumps of petrified trees encased in iron cages dot the desolate landscape. This unlovely geological cemetery is, for me, pure magic. I have always been fascinated by the ancient convulsions of the earth. A security guard notices my inordinate interest and comes over to share his knowledge.

'It's over one hundred and eighty million years old,' Jagat Singh says, pointing to a large petrified trunk. 'And these hills are relics of a range that is older and was once very much higher than the Himalayas.' I look dubiously at the stunted hills. 'A great sea once washed against them, rolling in from the west.'

The land was repeatedly submerged and thrust up again in those turbulent times and a series of inland lakes were formed. For thousands of years the atmosphere was humid and wet, and great forests flourished here. But the climate fluctuated. Dry winds sucked the life from the vegetation, and the lakes dried up. The sand from their beds blew in the howling wind, and the region became arid and hostile. Shepherds drifted in to graze their flocks and slowly the area was colonised. Why, I cannot begin to imagine. Rain clouds seldom deposited their moisture here, and drought was a way of life.

'I can remember,' Jagat Singh recalls, 'when children of twelve and fourteen rushed indoors crying in fear at the sight of rain which had not fallen since they were born.'

In years when the people escaped drought, great rustling hordes of locusts that bred in the desert descended on the land. Famine, too, became a way of life. 'We used to say that Bhukhi Mata, the famished goddess, has a particular affection for Jaisalmer. It is said that her legs are in Jodhpur, but her head is in Jaisalmer. One year in three drought, one year in eight famine – that was the norm. Recently, between 1968 and 1972, the rains failed in Jaisalmer for five consecutive years.'

Jagat Singh invites me to have a cup of tea in his hut near the entrance to the fossil park. He is a Bhatti Rajput, a hardy race bred by the harsh environment to be able to walk forty kilometres a day subsisting on only a daily handful of parched lentils and a cup of water for weeks at a stretch. Their only sustainable livelihood was plunder.

'We were feared throughout the desert,' Jagat Singh says with a rakish grin as he sits me down in his shack. 'When my ancestors entered a village, all the houses were bolted and barred.'

Closer to Jaisalmer, several Army and Border Security Force encampments are reminders that this is a border district where war is a perpetual possibility. There are also the everyday problems of arms and heroin smuggling to contend with.

I watch eagerly for my first sight of Jaisalmer fort, which travellers throughout the centuries have marvelled at. Described as the work of angels, fairies and demons, it emerges from the horizon like a mirage, towering above the stark flatness which surrounds it.

My first stop in Jaisalmer is the office of the Deputy Director of the Desert National Park. Naval is a harried man who hates being in town and is about to leave for the park. 'We have been criticised,' he says angrily, 'for the lack of animal sightings in the park and I am going to video whatever I can see in one evening.'

My request that I accompany him takes him by surprise. 'But there are no facilities, Madam. We have no residential arrangements, especially not for ladies.' I ask if there is a place where I can roll out a sleeping bag, and against his better judgment Naval is talked into taking me along.

I pile into his jeep with a photographer friend of his and various forest rangers and guards. We pass the dunes of Sam about forty kilometres out of Jaisalmer. The graceful mounds of wind-blown sand are awash with people: tourists, camel wallahs, musicians, hawkers of cold drinks and touts of every kind.

Many years ago I took a camel out into the dunes of Sam one night. It was a full moon and there was just me and the silver desert. I remember the shining sand, and the immense silence broken only by the chittering of unfamiliar insects. This pure, unsullied world is now defaced by litter, and the increase in tourist traffic is beginning to compact the dunes.

A patrolling police jeep flags us down as we near the Desert National Park. This is a sensitive area, close to the border with Pakistan, but the policemen recognise Naval and wave us on into the park. Gold grass, grey earth and the olive green of the odd bush or tree undulate into the far distance, back lit by the declining sun. The eye, by now accustomed to the absence of colour in the landscape, begins to respond to the subtle gradations of beiges and browns.

Chinkara, untroubled by our jeep, graze in large herds, looking up at us with large brown eyes. Giri, the photographer, films them, as well as the wild boar that snuffles up, appraising us with beady eyes. Black buck with dramatic facial masks and glossy black coats also linger to have a look, and then bound away, leaping as though they had springs on their hoofs.

What we are especially looking for is the greater Indian bustard, known to the locals as the *guhran*. Naval and Giri have told me repeatedly that it is a big bird, about a metre high with long legs and weighing about twenty kilos. Naval explains that the popular game bird has been hunted almost to extinction, and that the park is one of the few areas in Rajasthan where it can be seen. I scan the tall grass carefully as we slowly drive along the park's sandy tracks, raising clouds of dust as we pass.

A forest ranger taps Naval on the shoulder and points. Everybody gesticulates excitedly but without a sound, and I seem to be the only one who can't see the bird. Naval drives in the direction of the sighting and then I spot it – a big, sandy-coloured bird with a long neck. As it emerges from the undergrowth to browse on grass seeds, Giri leans out of the jeep, alternately taking photographs and filming with his video camera.

'They are usually found in pairs,' says Naval, and on cue the second bird appears. A third and fourth follow. Giri nearly falls out of the jeep in excitement. The birds run faster to gain momentum and take to the air, their big wings flapping in slow motion.

The forest checkpoint where we will spend the night consists of a few round mud huts. The Milky Way blazes across the night sky like the beam of a searchlight. The only electric lighting in the vicinity is at Jaisalmer, which lies beyond the horizon and doesn't intrude upon the darkness. This is the glistening galaxy of my childhood, a spectacle no longer experienced by city children because of air pollution and the glare of electricity. It is possible that this great display of stars will one day be all but obliterated even here, and the healing peace of the night will be lost.

The hut is snug and I fall asleep watching the reflection of the campfire on the gold thatch. I am up in the early morning to a grey, cold light. The world is empty and completely silent. Slowly and almost imperceptibly pink washes across the sky, and the birds rustle out of their sleep. Birdsong swells as the sun slips above a ridge in the east.

Camels arrive to take us into the park's especially protected core area. I don't think I shall ever get used to the lurching movement a camel makes as it gets up onto its feet, but once I'm up there I soon learn to sway in time with its lumbering gait. A pair of king vultures watch our approach from the top of a *khejri* tree. They must have a nest there, because the male flies off, trying to divert our attention from the tree. The female follows, but instinct impels her to sweep repeatedly over the nest. Spring is very much in the air.

Around a curve in the track, a sheep herder is grazing his animals in the park's protected core area. He is alternately apologetic and aggressive. 'I was asleep,' he says, 'and the sheep went in by themselves.'

'Then who cut the barbed wire?' Naval asks.

'Forgive me, sahib, just this once.' But Naval is implacable.

The herder retaliates, 'These lands are ours, they have been ours for countless generations. Just by putting a wire fence up, you think you can change the pattern of centuries. Anyway, what is more important: the survival of our sheep, on which the lives of our children depend, or some stupid birds?'

The approach to Jaisalmer fort is crowded with early-morning vegetable sellers, and I am greeted by the vibrant sights that I have now come to take for granted: veiled women with clanking silver and ivory bracelets, the colourful arrangements of fresh vegetables, a camel nuzzling a bunch of bananas on a barrow, a bull pilfering a bunch of spinach.

I am meandering up the road to the fort, the oldest in Rajasthan after Chittor, when I hear a rushing sound: it is water rushing down the drains of the fort, water from hundreds of taps and toilets as the inhabitants of the fort get ready for the day. My heart sinks. I wonder what such volumes of water will do to the fort's foundations, which were certainly not built with profligate modern-day facilities in mind.

Jaisalmer is one of the few forts in India which is still occupied, and the energetic if exploitative commerce of its inhabitants brings a special vitality to the city. Food stalls are already doing brisk business; I buy a mug of steaming hot tea and sit down to watch the morning unfold. Vendors drape their embroidered and mirrored cloths over every available surface. Shop shutters go up to reveal a formidable array of mineral water, cigarettes and toilet paper. A painted sign advertises a beauty parlour and its services: 'Purm, Padicure and Seissing'. A haze of dust and smoke from cooking fires makes everyday life in the town below the fort look mysterious and romantic, and buildings of yellow Jaisalmer stone rise out of the mist.

A passer-by who is curious about a woman, especially an Indian woman, wandering about Jaisalmer on her own pauses to talk to me. He is a Brahmin and lives in the part of town once designated for the priestly caste. He works for a government-run organisation which promotes the manufacture and sale of village-based hand-loom products, in continuation of Mahatma Gandhi's concept of rural self-sufficiency.

'Hand-loom cotton fabrics have now become fashionable,' he says, 'but we have been selling them for over fifty years. At first our main buyers were locals, but synthetics are catching on here and tourists are now our main customers. Foreigners have been through the cycle of synthetic fabrics, and are realising the value of pure cotton.'

He looks at his watch anxiously: it is time to get to work. 'It is a pity,' he says, 'that we cannot learn from the mistakes of the West, that we too have to go through the whole cycle before we learn to appreciate cotton. But even a son will not learn from the mistakes of his father, so I suppose we cannot expect one culture to learn from the mistakes of another.'

I leave my shoes outside Jaisalmer's complex of Jain temples and enjoy the feeling of the spotlessly clean floors, smoothened by millions of feet. There is an aura of serenity and the cleanliness is striking, in contrast to Hindu temples. A priest washes a statue, rubbing it repeatedly and devotedly to a high gloss. Over-the-top decoration no longer throws me after my experience at Ranakpur, and I am able to absorb the joyous celebration of life without intellectualising.

A Jain nun in spotless white pauses in deep meditation before a shrine. With her is a young girl of about fourteen who prays with similar concentrated devotion. They make a deep obeisance and move on. We keep passing each other, making eye contact and exchanging smiles.

Jain temples are important centres of learning, and this one is well known for its collection of ancient manuscripts, ranging from religious texts, astrology and traditional medicine to literature and political commentary. The library is said to contain over two thousand treatises – written on palm leaves, wooden tablets and paper – but it is firmly sealed with a heavy iron door, and is opened only once a year for fumigation. A few pages are displayed in glass cabinets: long, narrow palm leaves covered with script and illustrated with miniatures. They are around eight hundred years old. An attendant points out illustrations of a giraffe and a hippopotamus, depicted with realism and accuracy.

I emerge from the temple into golden sunlight, and find that the Jain nun and the girl have also finished their visit. Once again, we smile at each other. I hesitate to approach them, unsure about religious strictures, but the girl comes up to me, smiling shyly.

'Where are you from?' she asks.

The ice broken, we settle down on a wooden bench outside one of the houses nearby. But first, the older woman brushes the seat with a whisk of corded wool, the mark of a *sadhvi*, or Jain nun, to remove any insects that she might otherwise injure. The pair have walked to Jaisalmer all the way from Gujarat and are on their way to Delhi for a big religious gathering. They are barefooted to help them avoid stepping on insects.

The *sadhvi* tells me that Jain nuns have no homes, as they are on the move constantly, visiting places of pilgrimage and preaching. The laity regard them with great respect and the people from one village usually escort the *sadhvis* on the road until others from their next destination take over. Bhavana is the nun's niece and is thinking about becoming a nun too.

'Why?' I ask, addressing my question to the girl.

'You can't live in the world without sin. It is so easy to get caught in the web of the world.'

'What about your parents, your family? Won't you miss them if you dedicate yourself to this life?'

'I have my aunt, she is my guru and all the family I shall need. She is my guide to escape the world.'

The *sadhvi* looks on, smiling indulgently at a pupil who has learnt her lesson well. Bhavana looks away. 'The only person I would miss is my sister. We are very close. But that relationship, too, I must abjure.' She continues earnestly. 'There are so many distractions in everyday life. Television, for example, and the things you see on television are not always good.'

Bhavana, I begin to understand, comes from an average

Gujarati middle-class family. Everyday objects are, to her, fraught with potential for sin, as almost all of them involve the taking of life. Millions of microbacteria breed in a fridge and thousands are killed each time the door is opened or closed. Switching on a fan takes millions of lives when the blades revolve. Electric light is harmful, as it roasts the tiny insects that are attracted to it.

'Most people don't realise it, so that's not so bad,' Bhavana reassures me, 'but people like me, when they know of the pain and death inflicted by the most ordinary actions, cannot live with the guilt. So it is best to leave such a life.'

'We never bathe,' says the *sadhvi*, smiling gently, 'because water contains life. I haven't bathed for over ten years. And I wash my hands only occasionally.' I look at her disbelievingly.

'You will ask why we do not smell. It is to do with the purification of the mind.'

The period of Bhavana's novitiate will be at least a year. During that time she will experience the life of a *sadhvi* and receive instruction from her guru aunt.

'We take our vows as brides, wearing jewels and rich clothes. Not skirts and blouses, or even *salvar kameez*, but dressed in a sari,' Bhavana says eagerly. 'We are given a whisk like my aunt's and then we remove our jewels and throw them into the congregation. Then our hair is cut for the first and last time. After that we have to pull out each hair by its roots. We do it twice a year.'

My expression must convey my horror. 'Only by pain and penance can you purify the soul,' says the *sadhvi* resolutely. There is some triumph in the way she enumerates the hardships she has endured. 'The most important thing is to overcome desire. If there is desire, you cannot attain release. And to overcome desire you have to overcome all attachment. I no longer know the meaning of human attachment.'

'What about your niece?' I ask.

'I don't love my niece, I just want her to take the vows and to find release. This is part of my duty as a *sadhvi*, to help others give up the world. To help them overcome attachment.'

Bhavana becomes impatient with our conversation and begins to fidget. 'I have some shopping to do,' she says in response to the *sadhvi*'s questioning glance. 'But I don't have any money.'

They both look at me. 'How much do you need?' I enquire.

'I just want to buy some presents for my family, a few key rings and decorative pens, perhaps.' I give her a hundred rupees and she returns a few minutes later with a handful of shiny presents.

I have heard that there is a temple in Jaisalmer dedicated to a Rani who committed *sati* not on the pyre of her husband, but on that of her brother-in-law, but when I ask people for directions, they are curiously unhelpful. Finally, I am told in a muttered aside to ask for the Bhattiyani Rani ki Chattri.

High walls and a firmly closed gate enclose a cool, leafy compound containing a couple of dilapidated temples. The keepers of the shrine belong to a clan of Muslim musicians called the Mangiyars, who are famed for their folk music and are popular participants in Rajasthan's many music festivals. This family of Mangiyars, however, has not yet made it to the big time, and continues to sing the ballad of the Bhatti queen for devotees.

Rustum has long, unkempt hair and an obsequious manner. He showers me with extravagant compliments: 'Your gracious presence has brought honour to our Rani. You are such a grand personage, your karma must be pure and good.'

A visitor to the shrine senses my discomfort. 'The word *mangiyar* comes from *mang*, to ask or to beg,' he explains. 'These people go from house to house, singing and paying lavish compliments to each group of householders. "You are like a Raja," they say, "your grandfather did such and such, you are blessed, you are brave and courageous, you are generous in keeping with the great traditions of your family." And the people give to them happily in return for their compliments. Mangiyar musicians are found in all the villages surrounding Jaisalmer. They entertain the local people, who are then responsible for seeing that they don't go hungry.'

Rustum is happy to oblige me with a rendition of the ballad of the Bhatti queen. He strikes up the rhythm on a drum and proceeds to sing the story of the Jaisalmer princess who married the Raja of Jalore. It's a long and involved story, made longer by an extremely agitated lady who repeatedly interrupts him.

I eventually ask the woman to enlighten me on her strange behaviour. She explains that to say that the Rani became *sati* on her brother-in-law's pyre is to imply an adulterous relationship that is a stain on her memory, and so she is trying to stop the singer from singing the part of the ballad pertaining to the brother-in-law. Every time he says the word 'brother-in-law', the woman smacks herself on the mouth and then bends in apology to the shrine in case the Rani, who is a very powerful and vengeful deity, is affronted.

'The Rani was very beautiful,' sings the Mangiyar, 'so beautiful that all the other ladies of the harem became jealous of her. They gave her poison but she was so pure that it had no effect. One day her husband and his younger brother went to battle. The younger man was killed on the battlefield, and when his body was brought back, the Rani, who loved him as a son, became crazed with grief and ascended his funeral pyre.'

The possibility of a love affair occurring between a young bride and her husband's younger brother is a popular theme in many folk songs, particularly the more ribald ones. The bride did not have to keep *purdah* from him, since he was not an elder of the family, and so she had a more informal relationship with her brother-in-law than she could ever hope to have with her husband, who in any case was often away for long periods of time. The younger brother was usually closer in age to the bride, and perhaps more fun, and a sympathetic relationship often developed between the two, sometimes leading to love.

One afternoon a sign displaying the acronyms STD and ISD catches my eye, and I take the opportunity to call Ajit in Delhi. We are both excited that my travels are nearing their end and that

I will soon be home. It is impossible for me to communicate the richness of my journey, but I am now tired of drifting through other people's lives, tired of the intense activity and temporary friendships, tired of moving on for the sake of the journey. I feel the need to stop travelling in order to absorb and understand what I've seen.

I've been searching for a grand finale that will somehow bring all the threads of my journey together, and have seized upon the idea of going to the desert around Tanot, a military outpost near the Pakistan border. My car has finally broken down, and it will take a few hours to repair it; and because Tanot is as close to the border as civilians are allowed to go, there is a curfew there at night. All things considered, it would be sensible to postpone the trip until the morning.

But I have the bit firmly in my teeth, and I am determined to go. I make several calls to various taxi drivers, and eventually an ancient jeep rolls up, with a driver of similar vintage. Udai Singh eyes the conveyance dubiously and writes down the registration number. 'If you are not back by nine,' he says, loud enough for the other driver to hear, 'I'm coming out to find you.'

It's a much longer drive than I had anticipated, but that's also because Raifque Mia, the driver, watches his speedometer carefully and keeps below the forty-kilometre mark. I urge him repeatedly and politely to step on it; he nods sagely and continues at the same pace.

Raifque honks frequently as we pass by settlements, which are usually not much more than clutches of huts. 'I have friends in these places,' he explains, 'and it's important to stay in touch.

If I have a breakdown on this long and lonely stretch, I'll have them to fall back upon for help.'

He also honks every time we pass a shrine – Hindu or Muslim – and folds his hands and bows his head. It is an alarming habit, as he never slows down, but it endears him to me. It reinforces the continuing tolerance of India, the reverence for all gods. This was once standard in the subcontinent, before religion entered politics, before Partition.

There is something particularly stirring about the idea of heading for the border. Part of it has to do with my army-brat background and my strong response to military traditions. But I think it also has something to do with the defining nature of borders, the transition between one country and the next. This is a recent border, however, drawn arbitrarily in 1947; before Partition, the sandy wastes of the desert were considered as one region, populated by the same people.

We detour onto a sandy diversion where a bridge is being built over a branch of the Rajasthan Canal. The future waterway is full of sand blown in from the encroaching desert, but once it becomes operational it will change this land forever. I scan the horizon eagerly for my first sight of sand dunes, and slowly the landscape begins to change. First hillocks and then great mountains of sand tower on both sides of the road and appear to stretch for miles.

But every single one of the dunes has been planted. It would seem that the expanses of treeless sand I have seen pictured so many times are not in my karma. But my initial disappointment gradually gives way to the realisation that before the planting, this must have been a terrifying land: the dunes would have shifted regularly; paths navigable one day would have vanished the next. And for those who survived the terrain, there were the bandits, whose own survival relied on looting and killing. There was never any romance – only incredible hardship, terror and death. I realise the foolishness of using a single photographic image as an icon for an entire geographical area; and what is more, I realise the stupidity of romanticising such an image.

We drive on endlessly without passing a single person – an eerie feeling for an Indian. The dunes are higher now, and as we reach the top of one of the highest, finally, after weeks of travelling through Rajasthan, the landscape I've been searching for unfolds: for as far as the eye can see, there is nothing but an immensity of sand beneath a white sky. The sun is reflected off the sterile expanse, and the glare sears me, body and soul. The grand austerity of nature's bounty withdrawn cuts humanity down to size. I am intoxicated by the terrible beauty before me.

I think back to the nomads I have met on my travels, and their search for words to describe the desert. It is like the goddess, one of them had said, enormously beautiful but fierce and terrifying. Nothing could survive out here, and for the first time I truly appreciate the fortitude of the Rajputs. It was this harsh land that bred the endurance and courage they needed to conquer further handfuls of dust from which they could scratch a living.

We finally reach a small valley, with a temple and a tiny lake. Raifque grunts in satisfaction: 'We are getting close to Tanot now.'

My destination turns out to be a small settlement: just a few tents and a couple of barrack-type structures. Some soldiers are clustered around a tank near a small temple, sluicing off the day's dust before joining the evening worship. Their initial reticence disappears when I reveal my army background, and they slowly begin to tell me about their duties, which are largely concerned with preventing smuggling across the border.

'The problem is that the local people don't even think of their activities as smuggling,' says a man with sharp Rajput features and the usual handlebar moustache. 'They have carried goods back and forth across the desert for centuries. They've never thought of the desert as belonging to India or Pakistan: it is simply their homeland. The concept of a border means nothing to them.'

'The shepherds are big offenders,' adds another solider, 'because they get excellent prices for their sheep and camels in Pakistan. And they often bring back opium and heroin. They have been involved in the opium trade for centuries.'

Suddenly, the temple bells ring out for evening worship, and almost simultaneously the staccato chatter of rifle fire begins: a practice session has commenced nearby. The sun sinks slowly towards the horizon, and the sky is washed with saffron, the colour of renunciation, the colour worn by Rajput warriors to their final battle. The drab desert absorbs the radiant sunset, and I decide to head back to Jaisalmer before the indigo tones of twilight seep into the land.

On the final leg of our long drive we are cocooned in the velvety softness of the still night. Suddenly, in the distance, I see a collage of tiny pinpricks of light. We are not alone on the road any more: hundreds of milling woolly bodies block our path, and the silence is broken by the nasal whistle of the Rabari herdsmen who are trying to urge their flocks off the road.

As we draw closer, the mêlée of agitated shadows, surreal and elongated, is caught in the headlights of our jeep. The herdsmen are headed towards Tanot and beyond, and I am instantly caught up in the romance of their wandering lives. Even though my journey is ending, my restlessness is yet to be stilled. I wish I could cross the border with the herdsmen and see what lies on the other side. Once more I am seduced by nomadism: that fluid life, where it is possible to live out each fragment of time, each detour, without concern for conclusions.

GLOSSARY

ahimsa – the Jain tenet of non-violence
Akbar – one of the most famous Moghul emperors (ruled 1556 to 1605)
ashram – religious or community accommodation
Aurangzeb – last great Moghul emperor (ruled 1658 to 1707)

Babur – founder of the Moghul empire (conquered India 1526, died 1530)
Bahadur Shah Zaffar – last Moghul emperor (ruled 1837 to 1857)
Banjaras – nomad tribe, believed to be the ancestors of Europe's Gypsies
Bhairava – Bhil deity, also considered a manifestation of Shiva
Bhils – a tribal people of southern Rajasthan
Bhishnois – nomad tribe, known for their reverence for the environment
bhopa – Bhil priest
bidi – hand-rolled cheroot
Brahma – deity worshipped as the creator in the Hindu trinity of gods which also includes Shiva and Vishnu
Brahmin – member of the priest caste, the highest in the Hindu caste system

chadar – fabric coverlet offered by Muslim pilgrims at the tomb of a holy man

charan – bard whose verses preserve the unwritten folk history of Rajasthan
choli – cropped blouse worn by Rajasthani women
chula – mud hearth
Congress Party – (Indian National Congress) India's major political party, founded in 1885, which was the focus of the Independence movement and has continued to dominate Indian politics

dargah – place of burial of a Muslim saint
darshan – Hindu prayer service
dharma – religious and moral duty
dhoti – long loincloth worn by men

Gaduliya Lohars – nomad tribe, traditionally associated with blacksmithing and the Chittor area
ghee – clarified butter
gur – sweetmeat made from unrefined sugar

halwa – cereal or lentils fried and cooked in a sugar syrup
haveli – traditional town house with interior courtyard

Jains – adherents of an ancient Hindu religion founded by the twenty-four saints (see *tirthankaras*); Jains are traditionally in commerce due to their reverence for all living things (see *ahimsa*)
jali – intricately traceried window or screen
jauhar – ritual mass suicide by immolation, traditionally performed by Rajput women at times of impending military defeat to avoid being dishonoured by their captors
Jehangir – Moghul emperor (ruled 1605 to 1627)
jootis – traditional leather shoes of Rajasthan, featuring curled-up toes

kaaba – sacred rats found at Deshnok's Karni Mata temple
Kachhwahas – Rajput dynasty which ruled Jaipur; they were the first Rajput rulers to form an alliance with the Moghuls

Kalbelias – nomad tribe, traditionally associated with snake charming

khadim – attendant in Muslim shrines and mosques

khejri – (*Prosopis cineraria*) tree worshipped by the Bhishnois

Krishna – deity worshipped as the eighth incarnation of Vishnu; Krishna is depicted in painting as the blue god, and his life story is told in the *Mahabharata*

Kshatriya – warrior caste

kurta – long cotton shirt worn by men and women

lehanga – flared ankle-length skirt, usually measuring nine metres round the hem

maharaja – great king

Marwar – kingdom of the Rathore dynasty, which ruled from Jodhpur

matka – pot

Meos – tribe associated with the Patan area

Mewar – the district around Udaipur and Chittor

Moghuls – the Muslim dynasty of Indian emperors which ruled from 1526 to 1857

odhni – long veil worn by Rajasthani women

paan – chewable preparation made from betel leaves, nuts and lime

pichwai – large traditional cloth painting hung in Krishna shrine

prasad – offerings of food to a deity; the offerings are subsequently sanctified and distributed to worshippers

purdah – the seclusion of women

pyjama – any loose-fitting ankle-length trousers

qawwali – Muslim devotional songs

Rabaris – nomad tribe from the Jodhpur area

Rajputs – members of the Hindu Kshatriya warrior caste, the royal rulers of western India; Rajput dynasties include the Bhattis, Chauhaus, Kachhwahas and Rathores

Rama – seventh incarnation of Vishnu, whose life story is the central theme of the *Ramayana*

roti – bread

sadhvi – Jain nun

salvar kameez – baggy trousers worn with a *kurta* or long shirt

sapera – snake charmer, whose skill is traditionally associated with the Kalbelias

sati – to become an 'honourable woman' by immolation

Shah Jehan – Moghul emperor (ruled 1627 to 1658); builder of the Taj Mahal

Shiva – deity worshipped as the destroyer in the Hindu trinity of gods; also worshipped as the creator in the form of a lingam

Singh – literally, lion; the surname of members of the Rajput warrior caste

Sufi – ascetic Muslim mystic

thali – large metal plate

tirthankaras – the twenty-four great Jain teachers

Todd, Captain James – employee of the British East India Company who first arrived in Rajasthan in 1778, and whose *Annals and Antiquities of Rajasthan*, published in 1829, remains one of the major Rajput histories

vair – blood feuds which can often span generations

Vishnu – deity worshipped as the preserver and restorer in the Hindu trinity of gods; Vishnu's nine manifestations have included Rama, Krishna and the Buddha

zenana – the secluded wing of a palace or town house reserved for the women's quarters

LONELY PLANET JOURNEYS

JOURNEYS is a unique collection of travellers' tales – published by the company that understands travel better than anyone else.

It is a series for anyone who has ever experienced – or dreamed of – the magical moment when they encountered a strange culture or saw a place for the first time. They are tales to read while you're planning a trip, while you're on the road or while you're in an armchair, in front of a fire.

Lonely Planet guidebooks have always gone beyond providing simple nuts-and-bolts information, so it is a short step to JOURNEYS, a new series of outstanding titles that explore our planet through the eyes of a fascinating and diverse group of international travellers.

JOURNEYS books catch the spirit of a place, illuminate a culture, recount a crazy adventure, or introduce a fascinating way of life. They always entertain, and always enrich the experience of travel.

FULL CIRCLE
A South American Journey
Luis Sepúlveda (translated by Chris Andrews)

'A journey without a fixed itinerary' in the company of Chilean writer Luis Sepúlveda. Extravagant characters and extraordinary situations are memorably evoked: gauchos organising a tournament of lies, a scheming heiress on the lookout for a husband, a pilot with a corpse on board his plane . . . Part autobiography, part travel memoir, *Full Circle* brings us the distinctive voice of one of South America's most compelling writers.

WINNER 1996 Astrolabe – Etonnants Voyageurs award for the best work of travel literature published in France.

THE GATES OF DAMASCUS
Lieve Joris (translated by Sam Garrett)

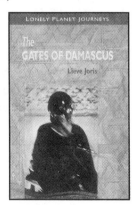

This best-selling book is a beautifully drawn portrait of day-to-day life in modern Syria. Through her intimate contact with local people, Lieve Joris draws us into the fascinating world that lies behind the gates of Damascus. Hala's husband is a political prisoner, jailed for his opposition to the Assad regime; through the author's friendship with Hala we see how Syrian politics impacts on the lives of ordinary people.

Written after the Gulf War, *The Gates of Damascus* offers a unique insight into the complexities of the Arab world.

ISLANDS IN THE CLOUDS
Travels in the Highlands of New Guinea
Isabella Tree

This is the fascinating account of a journey to the remote and beautiful Highlands of Papua New Guinea and Irian Jaya: one of the most extraordinary and dangerous regions on the planet. The author travels with a PNG Highlander who introduces her to his intriguing and complex world, which is changing rapidly as it collides with twentieth-century technology and the island's developing social and political systems. *Islands in the Clouds* is a thoughtful, moving book, full of insights into a region that is rarely noticed by the rest of the world.

KINGDOM OF THE FILM STARS
Journey into Jordan
Annie Caulfield

Kingdom of the Film Stars is a travel book and a love story. With honesty and humour, Annie Caulfield writes of travelling in Jordan and falling in love with a Bedouin with film-star looks.

The author offers fascinating insights into the country – from the tent life of traditional women to the hustle of downtown Amman. *Kingdom of the Film Stars* unpicks tight-woven Western myths about the Arab world, presenting cultural and political issues within the intimate framework of a compelling love story.

LOST JAPAN
Alex Kerr

Lost Japan draws on the author's personal experiences of Japan over thirty years. Alex Kerr takes his readers on a backstage tour, exploring different facets of his involvement with the country: friendships with Kabuki actors, buying and selling art, studying calligraphy, exploring rarely visited temples and shrines . . .

The Japanese edition of this book was awarded the 1994 Shincho Gakugei Literature Prize for the best work of non-fiction: the first time a foreigner has won this prestigious award.

SEAN & DAVID'S LONG DRIVE
Sean Condon

Sean and David are young townies who have rarely strayed beyond city limits. One day, for no good reason, they set out to discover their homeland, and what follows is a wildly entertaining adventure that covers half of Australia. Highlights include the weekly Hair Wax Report and a Croc-Spotting with Stew adventure.

Sean Condon has written a hilarious, offbeat road book that mixes sharp insights with deadpan humour and outright lies.

SHOPPING FOR BUDDHAS
Jeff Greenwald

'Here in this distant, exotic land, we were compelled to raise the art of shopping to an experience that was, on the one hand, almost Zen – and, on the other hand, tinged with desperation like shopping at Macy's or Bloomingdale's during a one-day-only White Sale.'

Shopping for Buddhas is Jeff Greenwald's story of his obsessive search for the perfect Buddha statue. In the backstreets of Kathmandu, he discovers more than he bargained for . . . and his souvenir-hunting turns into an ironic metaphor for the clash between spiritual riches and material greed. Politics, religion and serious shopping collide in this witty account of an enlightening visit to Nepal.

RELATED TITLES
FROM LONELY PLANET

Delhi city guide
Discover the seven cities of Delhi with this thorough and comprehensive guide.

India
This award-winning guide is the most detailed and comprehensive guide to India – packed with down-to-earth information and reliable advice for every budget.

Indian Himalaya
The vast Indian Himalaya has been an inspiration and retreat for travellers from Mahatma Gandhi to the Beatles. This guide provides extensive coverage of the region, from remote Buddhist monasteries to the hill stations of the former British Raj.

Rajasthan
Rajasthan, the land of the legendary maharajas, is India at its exotic and colourful best. This book is the most comprehensive guide available for the independent traveller.

Trekking in the Indian Himalaya
Experienced hikers and armchair trekkers alike can enjoy the splendour of the Indian Himalaya, from the rhododendron forests of Darjeeling and Sikkim to the high, windswept plains of Ladakh.

Bengali phrasebook
Order a meal, catch a rickshaw, chat with the locals – and do it all in Bengali with this practical phrasebook.

Hindi/Urdu phrasebook
This phrasebook, indispensable for travellers in north India or Pakistan, is packed with essential words and phrases and a useful vocabulary to help travellers communicate with ease.

India & Bangladesh travel atlas
Make your journey to the fascinating lands of the Indian subcontinent with the handiest, most reliable maps available.

PLANET TALK

Lonely Planet's FREE quarterly newsletter

Every issue of PLANET TALK is packed with
up-to-date travel news and advice including:

- a letter from Lonely Planet founders Tony
  and Maureen Wheeler
- travel diary from a Lonely Planet author
  – find out what it's really like out on the road
- feature article on an important and topical
  travel issue
- a selection of recent letters from our readers
- the latest travel news from all over the world
- details on Lonely Planet's new and
  forthcoming releases

To join our mailing list contact any Lonely Planet office.

LONELY PLANET PUBLICATIONS

Australia: PO Box 617, Hawthorn 3122, Victoria
tel: (03) 9819 1877 fax: (03) 9819 6459
e-mail: talk2us@lonelyplanet.com.au

USA: Embarcadero West, 155 Filbert St, Suite 251,
Oakland, CA 94607
tel: (510) 893 8555 TOLL FREE: 800 275-8555
fax: (510) 893 8563 e-mail: info@lonelyplanet.com

UK: 10 Barley Mow Passage, Chiswick, London W4 4PH
tel: (0181) 742 3161 fax: (0181) 742 2772
e-mail: 100413.3551@compuserve.com

France: 71 bis rue du Cardinal Lemoine, 75005 Paris
tel: 1 44 32 06 20 fax: 1 46 34 72 55
e-mail: 100560.415@compuserve.com

World Wide Web: Lonely Planet is now accesible via the World
Wide Web. For travel information and an up-to-date catalogue, you
can find us at http://www.lonelyplanet.com/

THE LONELY PLANET STORY

Lonely Planet published its first book in 1973 in response to the numerous 'How did you do it?' questions Maureen and Tony Wheeler were asked after driving, bussing, hitching, sailing and railing their way from England to Australia.

Written at a kitchen table and hand collated, trimmed and stapled, *Across Asia on the Cheap* became an instant local bestseller, inspiring thoughts of another book.

Eighteen months in South-East Asia resulted in their second guide, *South-East Asia on a shoestring*, which they put together in a backstreet Chinese hotel in Singapore in 1975. The 'yellow bible' as it quickly became known to backpackers around the world, soon became *the* guide to the region. It has sold well over half a million copies and is now in its 8th edition, still retaining its familiar yellow cover.

Today there are over 180 titles, including travel guides, walking guides, language kits & phrasebooks, travel atlases and travel literature. The company is one of the largest travel publishers in the world. Although Lonely Planet initially specialised in guides to Asia, we now cover most regions of the world, including the Pacific, North America, South America, Africa, the Middle East and Europe.

The emphasis continues to be on travel for independent travellers. Tony and Maureen still travel for several months of each year and play an active part in the writing, updating and quality control of Lonely Planet's guides.

They have been joined by over 70 authors and 170 staff at our offices in Melbourne (Australia), Oakland (USA), London (UK) and Paris (France). Travellers themselves also make a valuable contribution to the guides through the feedback we receive in thousands of letters each year.

The people at Lonely Planet strongly believe that travellers can make a positive contribution to the countries they visit, both through their appreciation of the countries' culture, wildlife and natural features, and through the money they spend. In addition, the company makes a direct contribution to the countries and regions it covers. Since 1986 a percentage of the income from each book has been donated to ventures such as famine relief in Africa; aid projects in India; agricultural projects in Central America; Greenpeace's efforts to halt French nuclear testing in the Pacific; and Amnesty International.

'I hope we send the people out with the right attitude about travel. You realise when you travel that there are so many different perspectives about the world, so we hope these books will make people more interested in what they see.'

– Tony Wheeler